Problem Gun Dogs

Problem Gun Dogs

How to Identify and Correct Their Faults

Bill Tarrant

Photographs by Bill Tarrant

STACKPOLE
BOOKS

First paperback edition published in 2002

Published by
STACKPOLE BOOKS
5067 Ritter Road
Mechanicsburg, PA 17055
www.stackpolebooks.com

Printed in the United States of America

10 9 8 7 6 5 4 3 2 1

First Edition

Cover photo by author
Cover design by Mark B. Olszewski with Caroline Miller

Portions of this book first appeared in slightly different form in *Field & Stream*, copyright 1974–1987 by CBS Publications, the Consumer Publishing Division of CBS Inc; and in *Field & Stream*, copyright 1988–1991 by Times Mirror Magazines Inc.

Also by Bill Tarrant
Hey Pup, Fetch It Up!
Tarrant trains Gun Dogs
How to Hunt Birds with Gun Dogs

Library of Congress Cataloging-in-Publication Data

Tarrant, Bill.
    Problem gun dogs : hot to identify and correct their faults / Bill
Tarrant ; photographs by Bill Tarrant. – 1st ed.
       p.   cm.
    Includes bibliographical references and index.
    ISBN 0-8117-1374-1
    ISBN 0-8117-2639-8
    1. Hunting dogs–Training.   I. Title.
SF428.5.T3815   1992
636.7'52–dc20
                                                                   92-936
                                                                    CIP

*For the little mongrel, Pooder (1967–1982),
and retriever champion, Renegade Pepe (1961–1976),
who made possible the insights, theories, and
training methods presented in this book*

Contents

Acknowledgments

I ACKNOWLEDGE A lot of people who have been a joy to my life and an aid in my career, which resulted in the writing of this book: John Bailey, Duncan Barnes, Nathan Barnes, Bill Berlat, Rex Broker, Bill Brown, Bill Connor, Jim Culbertson, Dog Writers Association of America, Omar Driskill, Danny Duff, Wilson Dunn, Queen Elizabeth, Chet Fish, Daryl Fitch, George Fossell, Mike Gould, Marie Graham, Hilliard Griffin, Sherri Haigh, Boyd Hamilton, Emory Haycraft, Jack Hays, Dale Lunsford, Doc and Ba Lyons, John McAssey, Bill Meldrum, Ron Montgomery, Bob Moore, Charles Morgan, Tom Ness, Margaret Nichols, John Olin, Outdoor Writers Association of America, Troy Parker, Lynne Peel, Cotton Pershall, Dave Petzal, John Pierce, Jim Pittijohn, Talbot Radcliffe, Bob and Willielee Ramsey, Bob Rathe, Jr., Ruby Ritz, Dick Royse, Gordon Sabine, Jack Samson, Glenn Sapir, Joe Schomer, Harry Schraeder, Don Sides, Delmar Smith, Terry Smith, Judy Stolz, Mary Suggs, Blanche and Bill Tarrant, Dee Tarrant, Sharon and Matt Treaster, Ty Trulove, Jean Wade, Ann Wagoner, D. L. Walters, Robert Wehle, Seymour Weiss, T. J. Whelan, Slaton White, Steve Worth, Watson Yoshimoto . . . and Jesus Christ.

Introduction to the Gun Dog

THERE WAS A town of my youth, where my father's kinfolk originated (incidentally, that town is now under a government lake), but anyway: there was a town of my youth named Delmar, Arkansas. And as towns would go in those days, Delmar had its village idiot. His name was Luke, and it would be a lack of taste if you asked if he were a direct ancestor of mine.

In the town of Delmar stood the village smithy under a great spreading oak tree, and as the smith would work, the ol' nesters would gather around and sit and talk and spit and draw designs in the dirt with a stick.

Well, this one day the smith had just drawn a red-hot horseshoe from the hearth and momentarily laid it on his anvil. Whereupon the village idiot entered, walked over, reached down, picked up the hot horseshoe, and in $1/10,000$ of a second flung the thing up, through, and out of the towering oak tree.

The nesters, with tears of mirth in their eyes, and slapping their knees with gnarled hands, shouted out, "It t'were hot, weren't it Luke?"

Luke appraised the lot of them but for a moment, then answered, "No, t'weren't hot . . . just don't take me long to look at a horseshoe."

Now, Luke had an ability that you and I as dog trainers don't possess. That horseshoe proved a problem for Luke, and he dispensed with it immediately. But when you and I have a dog problem, the thing can plague us for the life of the dog.

Of course, you might well ask, "Just what is a problem?"

And I'd answer you fast, saying, "A perfectly trained dog is that dog with only those problems you'll put up with." If the dog has a problem you can't stand – then that, my friends, *is a problem*. Which is to say, most every gun dog has – to some degree – one problem or another.

You can't throw dog problems up through a tree and be done with them – like the guy who had a problem he couldn't solve so he decided to forget it. No. Dog problems must be solved, and the doing so is the basis of this book and the vexation of all mankind. The reason being: it is much easier to avoid a problem that to correct one. But that luxury is past us: for here we deal only with dogs that already have a problem.

As the late John Nash, famous Irish setter breeder, handler, and trainer from Limerick, Ireland, once told me while hunting the peat bogs of Ballyfin: "You ever notice, Bill, there are no bad pups, just bad dogs?" John was observing the fact that most gun dog problems are man-made. Oh yes, some dogs can come into this world gun shy, bolters, hard mouth, biters, barkers, bone heads – but the vast majority of gun dogs (through selective breeding) come into this world well equipped to do the job God assigned them. But man screws them up. I'm not saying man does this on purpose. No, he does it by accident or lack of knowledge.

For example, take gun shyness. The dog is on point, the hunter brushes by, and his pants leg catches a twig to snap back into the dog's face just as the gun barks and the bird launches. Now in one second this dog may have become gun shy, man shy, bird shy, and cover shy. It was an accident. But like most accidents, it may take a ton of work to get the whole thing running again.

Traditionally, trainers have forced their dogs to obedience: be that hunting close, soft mouth, standing staunch to wing and shot, honoring another dog's work, what have you! And that force has been by hand. But I don't train that way. I train with the head, not the hand. I replace intimidation with intimacy. There is no such thing as a whip-run dog, so you'll learn nothing about that here. I won't shock, stomp, kick, cuss, beat, burn, shoot, whip, or torture in any way a dog to desired performance. And anyone who has this approach just don't have much fertilizer in their plot. In other words, their brain is sterile.

Now, you can gain a robot's performance – you can build a mechanical dog – through barbarism. But that dog has totally handed his self-will over to you and no longer relies on his natural senses to puzzle

A trainer takes time out for a love-trained dog: building the bond.

out a problem afield. Such a dog is worthless. The love-trained dog, on the other hand, works in compliance with the bond the two of you have developed, but he knows that in times of crisis he has the permission to turn the handler off and rely on his own good senses.

You'll notice this mechanical performance with collar-trained dogs when they are shocked to compliance with remote-controlled electricity. Such dogs will do the work—with their heads down, their tails sunk, and their spirits dashed. And let one go over a hill and find he's on his own, he goes berserk. All his self-will having been removed, he has no resource to forge ahead. But the love-trained dog will find himself in the same situation and joyfully fulfill the job.

My way of training is to enhance God's gift. The brutal way of training is to deny God and make a man-made dog. Even though the handler makes the mistake of saying, "By God, you'll do what I tell you or I'll beat you to death." It is not *By God* that he acts, it is *By Man*.

I don't know why modern man can't realize these gun dogs were self-hunting for millions of years—if not, how did they survive? If they had any built-in problems, they went hungry. Through survival of the fittest, man inherited a hunting dog that already knew everything afield to get a rabbit, coon, or bird. But man had to have the dog short-circuit this hunting act and turn the game over to the man to eat—instead of the dog getting a meal. That should have been simple enough, but then man started playing games. It wasn't sufficient the dog put food on the table, no; now he must put silver on the mantle. So man invented field trials, and the competition determined training – not common hunting sense.

No one ever put it better than Talbot Radcliffe, of Anglesy, Wales, world-renowned English springer spaniel breeder, who told me one day while we were training dogs on his 2,200-acre estate, "Field trialing is a game, you know, Bill? It relates not to the field, nor to game. It relates to man-made rules. To win the game . . . and I've always been good at that . . . you must play the game, you must know the rules, you must accept the sport of the game.

"It is not a hunt," he emphasized. "It is a game. For example, in this country we have fox hunting. And in fox hunting, we have point-to-point. Now point-to-point is to test the horse out . . . from point to point . . . in the fastest possible time. From that we have developed steeplechasing over made fences on a made course with proper jockeys.

"Now this steeplechase horse . . . you never take hunting. He is a specialized animal for specialized competition; a specialized game. You have a specialized sport, a specialized game, a specialized object. And to be successful in it, you have not got to go hunting."

Thank you Talbot, you put it all in a tidy nutshell. Which is to say, most gun dog problems are related to man's desire to enter competitions with his dog – not to go hunting with him. If it were just a hunting retriever we wanted, for example, we would cast the dog for the duck, and if he couldn't find it we would toss rocks at the duck's position. The dog would automatically go to the splash and find the bird. That would put meat on the table, but it could never be permitted at a field trial.

If field trials were truly designed to duplicate a day's hunt afield – which is their stated purpose – we'd have no problem. But this is not why field trials exist. They exist, instead, to show man's dominance over nature and beast. The dog will do as the man commands. The dog's innate instincts and natural ability are not tested. Instead, man's ability to get the dog to hand over his self-will to man is tested; to get the dog to trip over his own instincts: that's the goal.

Yet hunting, by itself, would exist to enhance those instincts. The dog that was prided would be the one who knew the territory, the quarry's habits, his location at any time of day, the best way to find him, approach him, and hold him for the hunter to take his best shot. And how many problems could such a hunting dog develop? Not many that mattered, I can assure you.

But with the field-trial game, we're always twisting and bending and breaking the dog to win the non-hunting game. Another example.

It takes a big-running bird dog to qualify for the national running at Ames plantation each February. That dog must qualify in championship events where he runs big, takes mile casts, always drives to front.

Yet, look at Ames plantation. It is pinched and crowded with foliage, and the dog cannot take a forward cast of more than a quarter of a mile (most times) and he's off course. And off course is a demerit. So man trains a big-running bird dog to qualify for the national running, but then must run him to death a week before the trail to shorten his race so it'll fit the constraint of Ames.

As a man who's spent his life with dogs afield, I could list one exasperation after another a poor dog must face on the field-trial circuit. And that's why dogs develop problems. But to stay on the circuit, those problems must be solved or the dog has no value. So he is then scrubbed out as a hunting dog. Which, *Eureka*, is the sole and express purpose for God to have put the dog on earth in the first place. So, you see the Catch-22! Only the failure gets to do what God intended him to do.

Well, enough said. I can tell you now we'll try to salvage both the bona fide hunter and the field-trial contender in this book. And the

The dog and man become one.

way we're going to do it is with personal influence. Mike Gould, the brilliant young retriever trainer from Carbondale, Colorado, expresses my philosophy well when he says his dogs are on an invisible elastic band. That is, Mike can control their actions by his will. He further says most gun dog trainers and hunters react to the dog's situation. The dog does well, and the man reacts by saying, "Good dog." The dog does poorly, and the man chews the dog out. But as Mike trains, the man acts, and the dog reacts. The whole system is just reversed. You can call it ESP if you want. And I had a discussion of this in *Tarrant Trains Gun Dogs* (Stackpole Books, 1989). I just call it all the result of intimacy in training. The dog and man become one, they operate on the same wavelength, they know what to expect of each other, and they proceed on mutual respect.

I'll give you an example of what Mike's talking about. His dog goes out of sight. Mike stops. He waits; within two minutes the dog reappears and reports back. The elastic band has stretched to its limits. Also note: Mike acted, the dog sensed this and reacted.

Of course, the only way this can work is man and dog must live together: twenty-four hours a day, day after day, week after week. You can't exile the dog to an outdoor kennel and see him only with a feed pan or a shovel. He gets like the abandoned bike in the carport: the tires deflate, the grease coagulates, and the exposed metal rusts.

All training must be based on a good foundation, so that's where we'll turn first. I once had an uncle who was always asking to borrow money from me. Each time he'd say, "I've got a million-dollar deal." And I'd say, "How much money do you need to invest?" "Ten bucks," would usually be the reply. Then, I'd tell him, "You got a ten-dollar deal if it takes ten bucks. You got a million-dollar deal only if it takes a million dollars."

Same with a dog. You can't build castles on sand—unless you accept the fact they'll be blown away by the wind or washed away by the tide. You've got to build on a solid foundation. You've got to build on a sound and sensible investment. It matters not how bold this dog may be or what predicament he's been placed in, there are ways to make him a performer. Maybe not a world-beater, but he'll be able to do the job you have in mind.

I'm going to tell you right now it takes tons of patience. And it means your turning yourself over to the dog, more than his turning himself over to you. It takes intimacy. It means bringing the dog into your everyday life. It means thoughtful observation and learning to read the dog and the dog learning to read you. Then and only then can we proceed. Okay!

PART ONE

THE DOG

1

Getting Started

WE'LL BE TRAINING two kinds of dogs in this book. Your own dog that has suddenly come unraveled. Or the newcomer, sent to you expressly to have you solve his problem. It matters not whether this dog is of your house or a visitor: they are both trained the same way. There is this one difference, however, and I'll not mention it again. Any time you bring a foreign dog on the property for training, that new dog must be kept in isolation from the kennel for thirty days to make sure he doesn't have an infectious disease that could infest all your home dogs. The newcomer's kennel must be located quite distant from your home kennels, for airborne spore can travel quite a ways.

At the same time, that first month of the dog's life with you will be the most important month in his training. We cannot train a dog until he trusts us, and he can't trust us unless he gets to know us, and he can only get to know us through constant contact.

That's why this dog should be the one that rides in the cab of your truck and sleeps beside your bed. Yet you must be fearful of disease and keep him from your other dogs. The problem with problems is they always beget more problems. You'll just have to work it out.

Also, how many professional trainers have had a dimwit come on their property with a scuttled dog in tow and say, "I'll give you one month to straighten him out."? The only person dumber than the guy with the dog is the trainer who would accept such an assignment. It will take at least a month for the dog and the new handler to become acquainted, let alone get to the dog's problem.

That's why trainers – not the owners – should always state how long correction will take. But the trainer needs the client (and he needs the money), so he tries the impossible. Instead, just hand the client this book and have him read the preceding two paragraphs. Okay! And dog trainers: stick to your wits. Don't be bulldozed into accepting an impossible task. The only way you could get done what the man wants is to brutalize the dog; in the end you'll have nothing except my anger.

And you who own the problem dog, you must heed this advice. It's your inclination to apply a Band-Aid where surgery is needed. You think you can get a whip or buy an electronic collar or shoot the dog in the butt with birdshot and all your problems will be solved. If those were the correctives for you, would you be solved?

Now your dog's screwed up and you'll have to step as far back in his training as needed to get to the basis of his problem. You may have six months' training in the dog, and it's all worthless. You must forgo those six months and start over: start from scratch. There's no other way.

A friend of mine is a psychoanalyst. He knows about my work and has remarked, "It may take years for us to help a person . . . but they expect you to do it in thirty days with a dog. Ha."

What we must do is modify the dog's behavior. We must re-create the dog in a new image. And this must be from the ground up. That's why we sometimes must return to basics: other times we can start building on what's good in the dog and just rearrange one niche of his behavior.

Oftentimes, we'll work directly with the problem. For example, with gun shyness we'll eventually introduce the dog to the gun. At other times we'll work indirectly to prepare the dog to more readily accept the gun. In this instance, the magic table. This may not be apparent to you at the time. In this regard, you'll just have to trust me. I know where the road turns, where the bridge is out, where the hobgoblins wait in ambush, where the ditches run with high water in a flash flood. Just let me be your guide. In the end, you and your dog will arrive at the destination of your choice.

Analyzing What We've Got

Newcomer or old-timer, we must first determine if the dog is ill. A dog with worms can really be thrown off his game, as can one with dermatitis, bladder stones, allergies, or any one of a thousand things. So get the dog to a vet for a thorough examination.

It may be that the dog's problem is his relationship with his handler, and that possibly will never be cured. Pity if it's your own dog. For a new handler is called for. Or you must now present a new side the dog's not seen before. But dogs aren't idiots, they can't be conned. They can see right through a sham as readily as I can see through a pair of binoculars.

The problem may not be you, but other dogs (or just one dog) in the house or in the home kennel. As long as this antagonizing relationship exists, there'll be nothing we can accomplish. And a dog's feelings can run deep. I presently have four Lhasa Apsos in the house with one West Highland white terrier. The Lhasas ostracize the terrier; that is, they just shut her out. And more than that, they'll try to nose her out of her bed space, her meal, her turn at the water bowl, her trying to get a ride in the family car.

I remember Scoop, a magnificent derby Labrador retriever who had it all. He was a large dog with a very dominant disposition, and I could have made a field-trial champion out of him—except he would never sit where his testicles would get wet. You can't place a retriever standing on a muddy casting line. They've got to heel, sit, stay. At the same time, there was a yard dog who hated skunks as much as I did, and it was his daily routine to dig them out and throw them twenty feet into the air until he'd reduced them to pulp. This dog was a 140-or-so-pound greater Pyrenees. His name was Moby because he looked like a great white whale. Moby and Scoop had a lifetime oath to kill each other. And on many occasions they tried to do just that.

Now Moby got along with the other twenty-eight dogs in the kennel and Scoop enjoyed all twenty-eight dogs as well. But there was just something about these two dogs where they could not abide each other. Each went to his respective death vowing to kill the other.

I had the same thing with an Australian cattle dog and a horse. The dog hated the horse and the horse wasn't about to put up with any nonsense from that dog. What a rodeo.

Laying out a Plan

When you've analyzed the dog, and you think you've determined his problem, then you must devise a plan of cure. It may mean working on just the one problem the dog displays; it may mean going all the way back to basics and reconstituting the dog. The basics are good, no matter what.

This is where you not only bond with the dog, but you gain the predominant status. You see, dogs are pack oriented. They fit into special strata. There's always a lead dog, and that must be you: the handler. But lead dogs are not made by force. What male couldn't whip the ordinary bitch? Yet the bitch may be the top force in a pack. We see it all the time with both domestic and wild dogs.

There are two reasons for this. Dogs, like humans, are sexual creatures. Sometime in that male dog's life he must come calling. Also, momma dog carries her young for sixty-three days. We now know there is cross-placenta behavior modification while the pup's still awaiting daylight. Then the average litter spends seven weeks with momma before adoption. So this is sixteen weeks of dominance momma has over every pup – male and female. I don't think the males ever forget it. They learned who they were and what was to be expected of them in the litter. And momma did it with mock malice – standing tall over the errant pooch, white canines gleaming, lips snarled back, eyes glaring, hackle standing straight up down her back, and that low guttural threat. There was never a bite, just a pretense or a presence. But, to my way of thinking, momma got her bluff in to last a lifetime. Therefore, the best way to continue a dog's training is to train just like momma. Mock malice. All huff and puff and no bite. Anyway it's worked for me, and through my *Field & Stream* gun dog column and several books, for thousands of others who have incorporated my philosophy and training methods. And it will work for you.

So, my inclination is to tell you to go back to basics no matter what the problem is. Get a handle on the dog, get to know him better, bond with him, and gain his trust. Then we can proceed to tackle what's really wrong.

Knowing the Dog

It will help immensely if you realize what an amazing creature you have in a dog. He is not a dumb animal. I am. The dog is always communicating; I simply can't decode one message. And he is always receiving communications. Subtle things. Things you never gave a thought to before now. And I can't learn how it's done.

Let's examine the dog. To put it all simply, a hunting dog exists to carry his nose. That's the apparatus that puts the birds in the bag. Do you know a dog has from 125 to 1,000 million smell cells? Man has about 5 million. I've witnessed, or heard of, smelling feats that have been mind boggling. Like the dope smugglers' eighteen-wheeler that came through Nogales and stopped at Casa Grande, Arizona. The sniff dog was brought to examine the truck. He walked as far as the saddle tanks on each side of the truck that were filled with diesel fuel and said, "It's here."

When the contraband was retrieved, it was found to have been wrapped, over and over, with layers of aluminum foil and gunny sack. The dog smelled the dope through aluminum foil, gunny sack, diesel fuel, and a steel tank wall. So realize: your dog can smell.

And what does he smell? Well, all his senses are set up to perpetuate the species, avoid peril, and get something to eat. Let's stick with the nose. The dog is especially critical in smelling butyric acid, which is a primary component of sweat. Tests have shown that dogs smell sweat one million times better than we do. And it's staggering to learn that the average adult sweats a quart a day. So the dog is intently tuned in to our mood. Should we enter stress and emit this through our pores, the dog has the message – and we didn't have to say a word. But having this message, the dog will now modify his behavior because he knows you have the possibility of going off the deep end.

In that regard, it's also interesting to note that the U.S. Army has conducted tests where it was learned dogs log a man's tired voice the same as if the voice were angry. Which tells us a lot about taking a dog out for training when we're pooped. Right!

Dogs have eyes that see movement, not detail. That's why they leap to the flushed pheasant, but may not have actually seen him: the nose told the dog the bird was there. But the dog does have superior peripheral vision: he sees from 250 to 270 degrees, while we can only see 180 degrees. So dogs catch things out of the sides of their eyes we never suspect they saw. Remember this. It's a major aid in training and understanding a retriever.

Ever come upon a rattled trainer yelling at his dogs? Well, dogs can hear very well. Especially a whistle. They have an upper limit of hearing that reaches 100,000 cycles. In other words, dogs hear ultrasonic sound.

And as for the sense of touch. How delicate does it have to be for a dog's coat to pick up static electricity that foretells a storm hours before its arrival?

But that's not all. Dogs are very bright. They can interpret us much better than we can each other. They seem to know what we're thinking. They can immediately pick up our mood. I've seen a house cleared of dogs just by entering angry and saying not a word. What did the dogs decode?

In addition, dogs are very sensitive. They're like women. They're intuitive. They can read our minds. Let me refer to my house dogs once again. (I've learned more about dogs from those in the house than I ever learned from those in the field. The reason is simple. I live with the house dogs and notice every nuance of their behavior, and see they notice every nuance of mine.) I'll be typing away and rise to get a cup of tea or go to the john and all the dogs will simply lie there. But let me rise with the thought of going outdoors, and they'll beat me to the door. How do they know?

The purpose of all this discussion of the miracle that is a dog leads me up to this one point. With a creature this bright and sensitive, there's no need to raise our voices nor our hands in training them. They know what we want, and we can get compliance better with kindness than we can with force.

2

Physical Characteristics

BEFORE STARTING OUR training, there's one last thing we need to do: look at the physical dog. Is he built for the job we have in mind? Will his physique permit him to do the work? What I refer to is functional conformation. Do all the dog's parts fit together to form an efficient animal, or do some parts restrict his chance for good performance?

Let's start from the ground up.

Feet

The gun dog's feet must be tightly compact so they don't splat on impact and sore the dog up so he can't get out of his crate to go hunting the next morning. Also, a splayed-out foot will pick up awns, pebbles, and burrs, which will further disable the dog.

The feet are the dog's natural point of contact with the earth. Do they have spring and bounce, or do they just flatten on impact? Also, how are the toes built? Do they fit to the foot like a cat's foot or a hare's? The cat's toes are compact and tight coupled, whereas the hare's foot is elongated. The elongated foot will give you speed from a dead stop, but it's the cat's foot you want for an extended race.

The dog's foot must also have high toenails. Low or long toenails

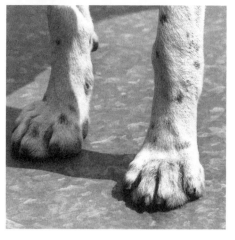

Job-rated feet: knobby tread, high toenails.

are more likely to strike rock and crack, split, or break. This will continually have the dog in a pit stop, getting repairs.

Forearm

The dog's forearms are another shock absorber; consequently, they must be angled to give and reflex upon impact. If the forearm is too straight, it transmits too much shock to the shoulders. A straight-legged dog will be so sored up by the second morning he won't be able to run; and if he can't run, he won't be able to take you hunting.

Length of Leg

If you have a dog that's short-legged in front, you end up with a chopped gait that sores the dog up in the elbows and the front end. Short legs in the back cause a hobby-horse motion that makes the dog bounce when he runs. Also, we must avoid the bench-legged dog, or one that's spraddled all out. Bench-legged back legs step on the front legs, so the dog shortens his gait to keep from tripping over himself. With a spraddle-legged dog, the legs are always winging. They naturally come up to the outside of the front elbows; consequently, that dog has a difficult time making a tight turn. Some dog men prefer a cow-hocked dog in the belief that when the legs reach and strike, they straighten out. Equally important, cow-hocked hind legs on a dog mean they place both feet near the same spot for propulsion. So they get spring and distance and balance. You know yourself you want both feet together when you jump. No way can you get any extension if you're jumping spraddle-legged.

Also, the cow-hocked leg straightens on push. It's like the thrust obtained with a pole while vaulting. If a dog can reach but can't push, he's a prancer. And if he can push with his back legs but can't reach with his front, then he literally runs over himself. What we want is a dog that can equally push and pull: now we've got a runner.

Hips

Hips are the ultimate shock absorbers as well as the primary hinges of the leg joints. If the ball of the femur slips from the hip socket, you've got hip dysplasia, which is probably the most disabling of all orthopedic problems. Consequently, only those dogs tested positive by the Orthopedic Foundation for Animals – a group that reviews X-rays and detects inherited hip disorders – should be put through training.

Neck

The neck holds the head. If held too high, the dog's neck, shoulders, and back will tire. If held too low, debris can more easily enter the mouth, nose, and eyes.

Eyes

Eyes and eyelids should be dark in color. This helps the dog handle bright sunlight. It also protects the dog from cancer such as you see in whiteface cattle. Equally important, the eyes should have a great bone balcony extended above them to knock away cover that could puncture, infiltrate, or irritate the eye.

Nose

A nose is a nose is a nose. It's the ultimate detector, the only way we have to locate most birds. Dogs are born with a good nose, average nose, or no nose. You can enhance a dog's nose through training with tons of birds, but you cannot really improve it. The dog's got what he's got. Yet you can destroy the dog's nose. One way to do this is work him a long stretch in very hot weather. The nose may be so affected it will never recover, and the dog never again will have that miracle sense of smell. It happens.

Ears

You don't want a dog with palm-frond ears; they're too likely to split when the dog shakes his head. And all dogs do it – especially retrievers when coming from water. Neither do you want a dog with a postage-stamp ear. That ear offers no protection from debris entering the ear canal.

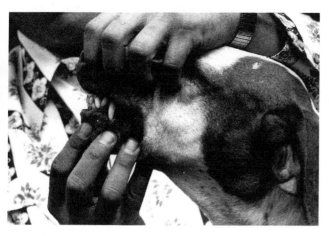

Bite is especially important for a bitch: she must gnaw the umbilical cord loose. Improper alignment could cause her to rupture the pup's belly.

Bite

How do the dog's jaws match? Are they perfect, undershot, or over-shot? A bitch with an imperfect bite can gnaw on her pups' umbilical cords at birth only to enter the belly and kill the offspring. And though dogs don't chew their food all that much – they mostly gulp even kibbles – have you ever noticed how a dog with a mismatched set of teeth usually needs constant tooth cleaning? And if you don't keep the teeth clean, they can go to pot, which can shorten the life of the dog through general body infection.

Skin

A dog's skin must be loose enough to spring loose from barbed wire, sharpened row-crop stubble, thorn bushes, and the like. If not, then the skin will tear. Also, if you think about it, the skin is the whole dog. It's the dog's house – his insulator, his protector, his bacterial barrier, and his thermostat. One vet told me the skin was the dog's largest "organ," as it is ours. Also, as I said up front, the dog's skin must be free of allergies and dermatitis, not to mention parasites.

Tail

We want a high tail – not for looks but for performance. The higher we raise the tail, the longer we extend the pelvic drive muscles – which give the thrust to the race – and makes a running hunting dog. And how does this come about? Well, the higher we move a dog's tail forward, the longer we extend the loin, hip, and thigh muscles: the drivers of the pelvic girdle.

High tail-set extends the pelvic drive muscles, giving the leg a longer and more powerful arc of the wheel.

Teats and Testicles

Bitches with long teats and dogs with elongated testicles are at a hardship for a day's hunt afield. The undercarriage takes quite a bruising on a hunting dog from stubble, briar, and twigs; anything protruding from that undercarriage is even more abused. You want everything tucked up tight, like a four-wheel drive with a skid plate. Nothing hangs down or it'll be subject to a beating.

Great Heart Girth

We're talking about the dog's life pump. The dog runs, his lungs and heart expand; if you've got a pigeon-breasted dog, there's no room to give, to expand, to accommodate the increased size of the organs, and the dog must stop his race or pass out. Yet, you don't want a barrel-shaped chest. That chest has reached its maximum. So you want a sprung rib cage where there's great elasticity, and the chest can expand or contract to the job at hand.

Now all this is related directly to the nose. A dog can smell only on the intake, never the outgo. If the rib cage can spring correctly, then the dog stays long-winded. The gaspy-breathing dog, however, will run right through a bird's narrow scent cone. The long-winded dog will be taking great intakes of breath and the narrow scent cone (the wafting effluva produced by the birds) will be detected.

So not only is the sprung rib cage the dog's life pump, it's also his air conditioner.

Brains and Trainability

I was just interrupted by a telephone call from a guy wanting a recommendation on buying a certain breeder's pups. The caller started talking about his own dog. "He's a swell guy," he said, "but he's so hyper . . . he just bounces off the trees." I told him what he needed was a biddable dog. That's a dog with lots of spring, but nevertheless he'll let you have a handle on him: like the accelerator to a race engine. You control the speed.

There are also dunces, and dogs so bright they should enroll in college. Bob Wehle of Midway, Alabama, the world's most successful English pointer breeder, says he can always tell a bright pup. The one, for example, that can figure out a gate. Others, says Wehle, can never get the hang of it, and just sit there and whine.

This photo shows many things: deep chest girth so Pup can breathe when hot, a mighty upper arm, and a good forearm for pull.

So let's hope the pupil you have before you is both bright and biddable. Frankly, there's little we can do if he's not. Oh, we can gain some control over any dog, but for the dog to control himself – that's the question.

High Pain Threshold

Remember years ago at the carnival the electric gripper? The device you gripped, where the current was gradually raised and you hung on till you couldn't stand it anymore? Stay long enough and you'd get a stuffed bear. Some guys could hang on and others couldn't. And it's the same with dogs. Some can barge pell-mell into a cocklebur field and just keep right on going. Others enter the same field and turn to stone. A high or low pain threshold is an inheritable trait. Once again, we have a situation where what you've got is what you've got. You can't improve it.

Endurance

Related to high pain threshold is endurance. Just what can the dog take? How long can he last? I'm not talking about the occasional hunter. I'm talking about the guy who's afield most every day from dawn till dark. He wants – he must have – a dog that can endure, that can stay with him, or more than likely outdo him. Once again we're talking about an inheritable characteristic. However, this is one trait we can greatly enhance – by roading him, by exercising him, by feeding him proper nourishment.

Conclusion

Now you know all the bells and whistles that must be connected with this locomotive of a dog. And you know about the pilot wheels and the drivers and the boiler itself, and the fuel and on and on. So we're ready to finally start training.

In this book we'll deal with bird dogs, retrievers, and flushers, and that can be done best by separating the book into three more parts. There may be some duplication, but that's fine. I firmly believe all gun dog trainers should be familiar with the training methods of other classes of gun dogs. In all my travels around the world calling on gun dog men (there have been thirty-three nations), I've come upon only two men who made up champions in more than one class of dogs. One man did it with pointers and retrievers, while the other man did it with retrievers, guard dogs, and herding dogs. Considering I've talked to thousands of gun dog men, I think the figure of "two" is staggeringly low. Don't you? We need to know what the other guy's doing, for his techniques have much beneficial transfer to our own breed of gun dog.

So let's get started. It all begins on the next page.

PART TWO

THE BIRD DOG

3

Correcting the Bird Dog

IT GENERALLY DOESN'T matter what fault the gun dog has, we must return to basics. That's because all gun dog training is like building a chain: you put link A into link B, and link B into link C, and so on. If you leave out a link, you have a busted chain; if you insert a weak link, you have a chain that can break at any time – especially during a crisis.

And that's what's happened to the problem dog. He must now be corrected because a link is either missing or weak. We may know exactly what link that is, but I've found it much better to return to the beginning and start all over. If the dog is essentially problem-free, he'll go through his basic drills in a day, a week, a month. But go through them he must.

He'll do it not only to prove to you he knows his drills, but to give him and you a chance to bond – apart from the crisis of his problem. Understand? To simply take a gun dog and ram him into a "cure" will accomplish something. That's for sure. It'll further drive the problem into the dog's psyche to the point where he may never be able to be cured. Remember, dog training must be based upon mutual trust and respect. It can work no other way. Yes, you can beat the dog nearly to death to get compliance. But the dog will work for you only out of grudge, not out of an exhilaration of spirit that comes from a love-bond dog that works to please.

So, we're ready to enter a humane training program. To start, let me explain three things: first, I call all dogs "he" be they male or female; second, I name all dogs Pup, even if they're fifteen years old; and third, when I train bird dogs, I'm including any dog that will point. When I train retrievers, I'm including any dog that will retrieve. And when I train flushers, I'm including any dog that will flush.

Breeds trained under the classification of pointing dogs are the weimaraner, vizsla, Brittany spaniel, small Munsterlander pointer, German shorthaired pointer, German roughaired pointer, German wirehaired pointer, Pudelpointer, spinoni, wirehaired pointing griffon, German longhaired pointer, large Munsterlander pointer, English pointer, English setter, and any dog that will point.

Breeds trained as retrievers include the Labrador retriever, Chesapeake Bay retriever, golden retriever, flat-coated retriever, curly-coated retriever, Irish water spaniel, American water spaniel, and any dog that will retrieve, including most of the dogs listed under pointers.

Breeds trained as flushers include the American and English cocker spaniels, Welsh springer spaniel, clumber spaniel, Sussex spaniel, field spaniel, English springer spaniel, and any dog that will flush, including most of the dogs listed under retrievers. And yes, some of the retrievers will even point.

The Basics

A pointer must be taught to heel. This will let you work him from horseback, Jeep, or by foot through a field-trial gallery, a pasture of cattle, an area near a busy highway, or around a section of country posted "No trespassing." Plus, this is the closest contact you'll have with the dog—except for teaching retrieve—and gives you the best chance to become acquainted with each other.

We teach heel with Mike Gould's power bar. Mike's a master retriever trainer from Carbondale, Colorado, and he's given us several beneficial breakthroughs in gun dog training.

We used to teach heel with a limp rope. But now we use the power bar because it provides us with a lever. A lever is a device that creates force by applying pressure at one end against the resistance at the other end; a fulcrum somewhere along the bar's length is the stationary point that increases power. Liken it to a leaf rake. A right-handed person holds the top of the rake in his right hand while the left hand grasps the rake handle somewhere along its length. The action of the two hands overcomes the force of the bent-back tines as they rake

Note: Text says to tie a knot in the cord as it exits the conduit. Here, Mike Gould has epoxied the cord in the pipe, so there is no knot.

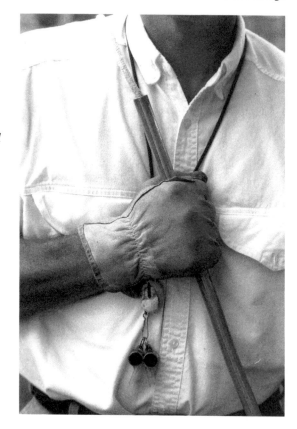

leaves, grass, dirt, or gravel. Great power is exerted to move the debris. So it is with the dog.

You build a power bar by cutting off a section of ½-inch electrical conduit. The exact length is determined by measuring the distance from the middle of your solar plexus to exactly six inches below your crotch. A twenty-eight-inch bar fits a man who is six feet tall. That'll give you a benchmark.

Now take a ⅜- or ⁵⁄₁₆-inch check cord and feed it through the piece of conduit. Slip it through a snap swivel and thread the cord right back through the conduit. Immediately upon exit at the top of the pipe, tie the end of the check cord to the main body of the cord with a granny knot. Tie it close to the pipe, and make sure to tie it tight: through use the cord will stretch.

Some twenty feet of check cord should protrude from the pipe. This you toss over your gun-hand shoulder; let it trail in the grass. In

Note: Text says to tie knot tight to bottom of cord around snap swivel. But cords stretch; that's why this one has a loose knot.

the photographs illustrating the power bar, you see a loop of cord some eighteen inches from the pipe. Mike uses this for extra power in teaching the dog to sit. I do not find the extra power necessary, so I omit it from my training program. Besides, pointer men (and women) usually don't want their dogs sitting. Incidentally, the end of the check cord is run slick – there is no knot.

So here we go. Attach the power bar snap swivel to the welded D-ring on the dog's flat collar. That collar may be constructed of leather or nylon (it makes no difference to us) but it must be stout. They cost little, so buy the best one you can find.

Okay. Clutch the top of the power bar with your gun hand in the middle of your solar plexus, place your non-gun hand either on the power bar or snap swivel, and step off, saying, "Heel."

If the dog balks, tap the snap swivel or bar with your non-gun hand. Note: I did not say *strike*; I said *tap*. You're generating great

The photographer has distracted Pup. When turning a right-hand circle, Pup's head should be parallel to handler's left knee.

When the power bar lies across the handler's lap, you know he's going in a left-hand circle. Note the cord dragging behind Pup. Keep going with the circle, and the cord will come up under Pup's tail, giving him further incentive to keep moving.

power, just a tap will do it. If the dog jumps to side, then tap him back to you. If he rears forward, then tap him back. If he crowds your leg, then tap him out. You have complete control – and again, you have great power.

Walk the dog in a great right-hand circle. Walk, stop, walk, stop. The commands for this would be "Heel," "Whoa," "Heel," "Whoa."

Now, reverse your direction and take the dog in a great left-hand circle. To do this, you'll need to change the position of the power bar. The dog will naturally crowd the leg of a right-handed gunner, so the dog must be pushed away. Lower the bar so it crosses your lap (which is now the fulcrum) with the right hand some six inches in front of your body and three inches off to your right side. The bar then crosses your lower lap and sticks out some distance to Pup's collar. Now repeat the walk, stop, "Heel," "Whoa," drill.

Encourage Pup with soft voice when he does well, telling him what a good boy he is. Say "No" when things aren't going right and give the bar the needed tap.

Interspersed with this drill must be a sweetening-up process. I call it Happy Timing; the dog is given free rein to hit the countryside (under your supervision) and do what he wants. Yet we can't take a bolter out and let him go. Bolting may be the dog's problem, so we must keep him on a check cord. Or carry lots of birds in our pockets to toss to the wind and coax Pup back to our reach. Remember, there's hardly a problem that can't be solved with birds.

But if the dog is not a bolter and you can keep some sort of a handle on him—which can readily be done by running him with a pack of honest dogs—then let him go. Nothing will do him as much good as a romp in the countryside, driving through brush, skimming over mixed-prairie grass, stumbling through ditches, and wading skim water, where he can leap aside from the toad's jump, the bullsnake's hiss, and the bull's charge. Pup must learn the countryside. He must run wild until his environment disappears. That way, there'll be no surprises. The twig's snap, the dickeybird's launch, the stench of horse

Note: Bird dogs are never taught sit *and* stay. *Instead they are taught* whoa. *Okay? But in this sequence of photos we'll run the retriever through the sit, stay, come process. Mike tells Pup to sit as he raises up on the collar-end of the bar and pushes the solar-plexus end of the bar toward the dog's head. Pup must sit. He has no alternative. Then Mike drops the bar, steps before Pup with his hand up like a traffic cop, and says, "Stay," as he presses the bar into the earth with his left foot. When Mike wants Pup to come, he gives that order and flips the bar up from its bite in the ground and reels the cord in hand over hand till Pup stands before him. Pay no attention to the loop in the check cord. Mike uses it to reinforce* sit.

The whole whoa post is depicted with post beat to ground, Pup wearing a cord from the whoa post to the "back" collar (the handler holds it in his right hand), and the check cord leading from the "front" collar to the trainer's left hand.

The handler heels the dog away from the whoa post until the dog feels the "back" collar pull when they take one more step: it will be taut between post and collar.

manure – all these things will have been experienced and no longer pose as a curiosity to divert Pup from his mission of concentrating on birds.

Plus, a good run will let him shake off the stress of the power bar. Yes, there is stress in any close drill. Recognize this, respect this, and let the dog shake it off by Happy Timing.

Whoa and Come

The power bar teaches more than heel and whoa (and sit and stay for retrievers and flushers). It also teaches come. Stand beside Pup as he wears his power bar, tap the bar back, and say, "Whoa." Then step off and immediately turn to face Pup. Stand directly before him, your face stern, your hand up like a traffic cop, as you continue to say over and over, "Whoa." Then drop the power bar so it wedges into the dirt and angles back up to the D-ring on Pup's flat collar. Keep stepping back, ever holding the rope, ever repeating the command "Whoa," ever keeping your face stern and your hand up like a traffic cop. When you reach the end of your rope, stand there a minute if Pup's compliant. Should

The handler takes that one more step as he commands, "Whoa." If the dog takes that one step forward, the handler yells, "Whoa," and either releases the dog to check-cord in the field and shake it all off or returns the dog to the whoa post and heels him out again.

If Pup goes belly-to-ground on you, pump him up as shown.

you see him start to move forward, then make his initiative your command and order, "Come," as you flip the power bar up out of the dirt and milk the check cord in hand over hand. Milk fast so the bar does not strike the ground and wedge Pup while he's running. That would be a catastrophe.

Keep repeating this drill, interspersing it with heel and Happy Timing. Or just tell the dog, "Hie on," and let him race ahead on the twenty-foot check cord to shake it all off.

But should Pup refuse to whoa as you step forward and face him, it's time to leave the power bar for a moment and introduce him to the whoa post.

The Whoa Post

Notice we're continually hooking links into the chain. We begin with one link, *heel*, then attach that to another link, *whoa*, which is attached to yet another link, *come*. So it will go throughout our course. And should Pup prove weak in any one link, then we reinforce that link with additional drills.

We build a whoa post by pounding a stake, a T-post, or a pipe into the ground so it is double stout. Then we outfit Pup with two flat collars, one next to the other. The collar to the rear is attached to a twenty-foot cord that is doubled back to loop over the whoa post. Consequently, the entire length of the cord from post to Pup is ten feet. Okay!

Now we attach another check cord to Pup's front collar. This cord we hold in hand.

All right, heel pup to the post. Then tell him, "Heel," step off, and start walking him away. One step before he hits the end of the whoa-post rope you stop, saying nothing. Let Pup collect himself, and then make that one step off that prompts Pup to step forward—and when he does he'll be at the end of his whoa-post rope, which will hold fast against his back collar as you (with absolute correct timing) say, "Whoa."

You then walk about and stand in front of Pup. Face stern, hand up, you walk away, holding the check cord and saying over and over, "Whoa."

Then you release Pup from the entire contraption and walk him a hundred yards around the yard and bring him back for a second drill. As with all training, we never persist in a drill; rather, we enter it, exit it, let Pup shake it off, then return for another go. We never drive Pup into the ground. We keep him up, keep him happy, keep him attentive. If you persist in drills to beget a lackluster performance, that's what Pup will transfer to the field. For we train as we hunt, and we hunt as we train. There is no other way.

So let's run through the whoa-post drill one more time. Pup is taken to the pole, you say, "Heel," and step off. This induces Pup to follow—and you keep looking back. When you see that one more step will bring the whoa-post rope to its end, you stop, saying nothing. Pup should stop, too. Then you let him collect his wits before you make the one final step that Pup will follow, and just as he hits the end of his whoa-post rope you'll say, "Whoa." Your timing must be absolutely correct. For all dog training is split-second timing. Late or early and you've blown the effect. You want Pup to get it right? Well, you've got to get it right as well. Which is amusing when you come to think about it. Men bring us dogs to cure of gun shyness only to find the man is also gun shy. Or they bring us bolters—and the men are bolters as well. Think not? You've got Pup in a pheasant field and he surges ahead, but instead of controlling him you increase your pace. So now Pup is bolting and so are you! This is when the dog is acting and the handler reacting. And it must always be the other way around. The man acts, and the dog reacts.

I mention in the text that you can take the power bar off the dog's collar and attach it twenty feet distant. This gives you a fulcrum for power-casting your dog across the field. Here, Mike Gould demonstrates how he can even work a cord with no bar attached to the collar and still get a lot of power.

By the same token, you see in this photo that Mike has no power bar on the check cord but here he acts as though he had a bar directly in his hands. He can then cast the dog in a left-right pattern before him, vacuuming the bird field. What it all boils down to is this: once you get used to using the power bar, then you can proceed without it.

Back to the Power Bar

So now it's back to the power bar. But one last thought. I've seen too many dogs go down on the whoa post. That is, they flat drop to belly. Well, we must apply reverse force when this happens. The dog's down, so we go to him and pump him up. How do we do that? Well, when you were in grade school some guy would pop you on the shoulder and you'd fall sideways. He'd pop you again, and you'd stand your ground. He'd pop you a third time, and you'd lean into the blow. Pup will do the same thing.

Just put your expanded hand over his flank and start pumping. He will come up just like an inflated balloon.

And while we're discussing reverse force, you'll also use this on the whoa post. Remember that check cord you have in hand? Well, when you're to front and Pup's whoaing, you say "Whoa" and tug on the check cord. This action wedges Pup between the cord you hold and the whoa-post cord that holds Pup fast to the whoa post. Keep tugging and Pup will rear back. Now you're reinforcing whoa. Nothing could be better.

If you want to enhance this even further, tie a bowline knot in your hand-held check cord. Place the knot just far enough from the snap swivel on Pup's D-ring so it lines up exactly with his bottom jaw. When you flip your hand to send a wave down the cord, the bowline knot will come up to slap Pup under the chin just as you say "Whoa." But again, we're talking split-second timing. You can't be late or early. And what's the effect? Well, the body follows the head. As the head rears back, the dog braces back, and just as the head comes forward, the dog leans forward. One is reinforcing whoa, the other is enticing Pup to break. So we continually snap his head up and back to set him solid on his haunches.

Then we apply reverse force and give short tugs trying to get Pup to take a step forward. But instead, he rears back. Hooray! Now Pup's really starting to whoa.

Okay, when this session is completed you can return to your power bar, step around in front, throw the power bar down so it wedges between Pup's collar and the dirt, and continually back off, saying, "Whoa."

Turning the Power Bar Around

Now we unsnap Pup from the power bar and tie a snap swivel to the opposite end of the check cord – the slick end, remember? We hold the power bar before us, but Pup is twenty feet away. We start by getting him to come to us and heeling him to side. Then we cast him to field. We're going to check-cord Pup into the wind, beating a path before us like he was lacing a hunting boot. Off he goes to the right, so we get our power bar across our chest, parallel to the ground, with the left hand sticking out as far as we can control the bar and still apply power. We say "Ho" to get Pup to turn around, or we blow a big Acme Thunderer whistle one long blast, and Pup complies. He turns to look. Well, we've got our left hand extended for a left-hand cast and we've got the power bar out there for added power, so we jerk it and step off to the left.

Pup crosses the field before us.

When he nears the end of his check cord, we again cry "Ho," or blow our whistle. Pup turns to see what we want, but now our bar is sticking way out to the right, and we give the bar a tug with our right hand—rendering a hand cast—and we walk that way and Pup complies. Now we've got him lacing the field. We've got him quartering, we've got him hunting, we've got him under control, and he's working within gun range. It's beautiful.

What's happened? With a handful of devices—a power bar, a whoa post, a couple of check cords, two leather collars, and a bowline knot—we've got Pup to answer to the commands heel, come, stay, and whoa; take a hand cast; quarter the field; and answer the voice or whistle signal. Plus, we've reinforced the most powerful command in dogdom, "No," as well as the most supporting, "Good boy" or "Good girl."

Did you have any of these problems: heel, come, stay, whoa, cast, quarter? Well, you just solved your problem. And you didn't lay a hand on Pup. You didn't shout at him, kick him, shoot him, shock him, or nothing. I call this training with our heads and not our hands. You might say we're no longer "Hand"-lers, we're "Head"-ers. We've got Pup moving with no grudge, totally compliant and up. In addition, we're sweat-free, fret-free, and positive about tomorrow, for all things are going to continue good and we know it. Pup's going to become a great performer.

And that's dog training, my friends, that's dog training.

For look at Pup. He's happy. We had to bond with him and we're doing it. He now feels our firmness, but that's mixed with a mellow kindness. He now knows he must do what we tell him to do, and each time he's brought along by being placed in a position to self-train. And that's what we'll continue to do: position Pup to self-train or have other dogs train Pup for us.

Which prompts me to mention this one thing. I know the amateur trainer is handicapped by not having a kennel full of dogs: it's easier to train thirty than it is one. But at the same time, the pro has much to do, so he can't concentrate on one dog the way you can. So you've both got troubles, and you've both got benefits; each of you has to work things out for yourself.

The amateur needs to join a gun dog club where handlers meet to train their own dogs with your help. In return, they spend time helping you. And the pro? Well, he needs to either innovate or make enough money to hire help. But by the same token, many pros are pleased to see a dedicated amateur come on board. You do a day's work for the pro, and he helps you train Pup.

Professional trainer Tom Lovett takes a day off and hunts five gun dogs on blue grouse. Note the relaxed composure of dogs and man. All of them honor each other and the bird.

Finally, the most important thing accomplished in this chapter is Pup is bonding with you as the handler. Nothing else can be more important. You cannot force any living thing to do anything. But you can position them where they want to comply. And when successful – when he sees the delight this has brought to you, and in turn being fussed over and petted and encouraged to keep on doing right – the Pup will be a willing student. And that's all we can ask from either man or beast, isn't it? You bet your shotgun it is.

4

Wing and Shot

THERE IS A truth in dogdom: *there's not a problem a dog has that can't be solved with birds*. Now birds are our subject. And I'd like to handle several things at one time, but there's no way it can be done. For we need to consider birds, guns, the whoa post, the chain gang, the walking chain gang, and the feather dance all at the same time.

Well, let's start somewhere. You and Pup have been on the whoa post—which has nothing to do with birds. *Whoa* simply means, "Put all four feet flat and don't move a muscle, not even an eyelid." Repeat, whoa has nothing to do with birds. It's a command that can be given any time you want Pup to stand immobile. And I'm mighty glad it sounds so much like "No." For it practically means the same thing. Pup's about to enter a waste-disposal pit, or run out on an interstate, or chase down a calf. No and whoa will stop him in his tracks.

So, how do we apply whoa to birds? In other words, how do we get Pup to honor wing and shot? There are two conflicting ways, and I'll explain both.

First off, we use our present equipment: the strong, flat collar with welded **D**-ring and twenty-foot check cord. Remember: all dog training is connecting links in a chain.

Okay. We prepare a bird field by mowing all about and leaving tall tufts of grass, or we use the grass as is and pile up bunches of bushes or branches. Now we have a point of destination, what dog handlers call points of opportunity. These look like birdy places where a skilled Pup would automatically run. We plant birds in these places, but we don't dizzy them to put them down. There are two reasons for this. First, it takes skilled hands to plant a bird so it arouses at the precise moment needed. Second, when dizzying a bird you make him practically comatose; furthermore, you place the bird's head under his wing and put that wing to earth. And this, my friend, has denied the dog a source of scent: the bird's breath. Yes, bird dogs cue on bird breath (and bird droppings) as much as they do the effluvia (an outpour of airborne particles given off by the bird's body). So, I repeat, we don't dizzy and plant the bird. But we do immobilize him for two reasons. First, it gives us a chance to present Pup a feather dance; and second, it allows a short, fascinating flight that Pup can mark down either to hunt up again or in actual hunting fetch deadfall.

Hobbling the Bird

We use the common barnyard pigeon, for he's the heartiest and stinkingest of all training birds. Don't worry about transfer from

Pigeon hobble is made with a section of discarded garden hose with a nock cut in one end. Three feet of ⅜-inch nylon cord is run through the nock and tied off. Each cord goes to one of the bird's legs and is tied just tight enough so it won't slip or chafe. Don't worry about the pigeon: I've had 'em die of old age in my coop. The bird is picked up to present to the dogs by grasping the hose and letting the pigeon fly with the wind.

Handler check-cords Pup into planted bird's scent cone. When Pup makes game, the handler rushes forward (silently) and positions himself as shown.

pigeons to gamebirds: your dog can make the switch without a hitch. Take the bird dog pros that summer on the North Dakota and Canadian prairies. They train on sharptail grouse and Hungarian partridge. Then comes the fall Dixie circuit on bobwhite, and the dogs make the transition with no problem.

Our hobble is a section of discarded garden hose, say eighteen inches long. You'll learn through practice what length you want for the job (or the dog) you have at hand. Now nock the hose on one side about ½ inch down. Take a piece of ⅛-inch nylon cord, and tie it to the hose so you have two equal lengths hanging down. Then tie each length to each leg of the pigeon. Use whatever knot you prefer, but be careful not to make it so tight it impedes blood flow. You also don't want it so loose that it either chafes the pigeon's legs or flat comes off. Remember, we'll be using each pigeon hundreds of times.

Place the pigeon in the tuft of grass or brush pile. Use as many birds and as many points of opportunity as you want.

Go get Pup, snap on your check cord, and quarter him into the wind. The moment he makes game (detects a bird's scent cone), Pup's disposition and his body will change. You need to recognize this and act accordingly. His ears will come up, his nose will jut out, and his haunches will turn rigid or tremble. Either his front legs grow post-legged or he tries to bolt. When you see Pup strike game, secure the

The bird boy skirts handler and dog and goes to lift the bird and give the dog a feather dance. Handler holds tight, and bird boy (Ty Trulove) hurrahs as he lets the bird fly with the wind. Weighted bird has slow flight, so the dog can mark him down and either go to him and point him once more or, in a hunting situation, go and fetch the deadfall.

check cord with both gloved hands and walk down the cord hand over hand, ever keeping the cord taut. Don't let Pup move a foot; he's on whoa, and that's what whoa means. Only we don't say whoa. We say not one word. We also move slowly and deliberately. We try to disappear as much as we can. We must not do anything to break Pup's concentration or in any way turn his head from the bird.

This is Pup's most important moment of truth. Let that truth be all his – don't interfere. When you've reached Pup's side, kneel down in a very precise way. Say you're a right-handed gunner. Approach pup from his right side, then drop to earth as follows – ever keeping the cord taut. Drop your left knee flat to earth, bend your right knee, and plant that foot hard. Then take your left hand and circle it about Pup's waist while your right hand grasps the flat collar. Now you've got Pup. He can't move and he surely can't bolt. Should he try to move left, the left arm will secure him. Should he try to bolt straight ahead, both arms will hold him. Should he try to rear back, the right hand will stop him. Should he try to crowd your left side, your flexed right leg will dig in and hold him.

The Bird Boy

Immediately upon getting Pup anchored, a bird boy appears from behind and enters the tuft of grass or the stack of sticks. He reaches down and takes the far end of the garden hose in hand and lifts up the bird to catch the wind. The bird's wings will slap, and the bird boy will make that sound of flushed quail with his mouth *(burrr-rrrrrrrr)*. He'll do this over and over. This is the feather dance, and Pup will be more attentive than a sailor on his first shore leave in a year watching the gal on stage wave her boa.

Suddenly the bird boy throws the pigeon with the wind while he fires a .22 training pistol, and all Pup breaks loose. I mean, you've got whimpering and rearing and lunging and dropping flat-butted and digging in and frothing and looking glass-eyed and trying every way possible to get that bird. But you say nothing, you do nothing, except hold on. Pup's just stood to his first wing and shot, and it came off perfect. He honored the bird's scent (he found the bird), he saw it presented and fly away, and he's just confirmed his being: he's a bird dog.

But one minute. If you don't think Pup's ready for the sound of that .22 training pistol, then just have the bird boy make a *pow* sound with his voice when he launches the bird. Okay?

There's another way to go about all this, too, and it is popular with some pros. They get lackluster performers in training, plus those who have never been Happy Timed, so they have to pump up the pupil. Consequently, they take him to field on a check cord, dizzy the bird, have a bird boy kick it out, *and let the dog break and chase.* This is not my way, nor should it be yours. The pro must still break the dog to wing and shot.

If we have a lackluster dog, we go to the chain gang.

The Chain Gang

This is the first time we'll have the opportunity to let other dogs train Pup. If Pup is not interested in birds or if he's man shy, gun shy, or cover shy, put him on the chain gang. It is a powerfully wonderful tool that has salvaged more dogs than probably any other device. What happens is this: The disinterested dog is placed on a semi-rigid chain with all the dogs the handler can attach. When one dog moves, all dogs move. In other words, they're all learning to give to the lead. When you introduce something to excite all the dogs – like a bird flown right over the bunch of them – the entire gang goes berserk. This builds interest, with the by-products of boldness, intensity, birdiness, and most important, *envy*. Leave the errant pooch on the chain gang long enough, and he'll strive to get into the game. He wants the fun he sees the other dogs having. He wants to be one of those dogs, which is to say, he wants to be a performer.

We build a chain gang as follows. If you're in the dog business, you'll want a chain to house eight dogs, or 49½ feet long. If you're only interested in creating an effect and you've got to borrow the neighbor's dogs to do it, then you need a chain 27½ feet long to accommodate four dogs. Here's our spacing. Because dogs go berserk on the chain and could end up fighting each other, there must be 66-inch spacing between occupants. Plus, you need two more segments of 66 inches at each end of the chain.

At each end of the chain gang, you attach a large O-ring. Through these drive two circus stakes. Drive them stout and make sure the chain is semi-taut. At 66-inch intervals, attach an 18-inch-long chain (the drop line), snap-swiveled top and bottom. We now have what resembles a trotline used to catch catfish.

To each drop line we attach a dog. They'll resent it, I'll assure you. And since we're never a part of a dog's plight, we walk off and leave them – we get entirely out of sight and let them go at it.

We must make sure, however, that our chain gang is in the shade, especially on a summer day, and we must return every hour to give water. Talk to the dogs soothingly, let them know you are in no way connected with what bothers them. Matter of fact, tell them that by

Here we have a typical chain gang filled with pointers.

This Y-connector lets one helper handle two dogs at the same time. In the photo on the next page, the training camp has three handlers for the walking chain gang: one handler for an all-age dog and one handler for each of the following dogs.

saying, "Why, what's this, Pup? You all tied up? And these guys are jerking you around? Well, isn't that a shame?" Then get out of sight.

I've seen first-timers put on the chain gang that could teach the Olympic acrobatics team a move or two. And I've seen old chain-gang veterans that dig a cool hole to rest in and go to sleep.

Leave Pup on the chain gang a while, and then put him away.

Bring him back the next day for more of the same.

And the next day.

Finally, while all the dogs are chained, we'll bring an all-age dog into view, have the bird boy loft a bird, and let the dog run to chase the hobbled bird down (we'll fire a gun only if there's no gun-shy dog on the chain gang). Will this excite Pup? You bet it will. Then stand at one end of the chain gang and loft a bird to fly over the lot. You're using a homing pigeon now that will just fly back to its loft. As the bird passes over, there'll be leaping and lunging the likes of which you've never seen. And what's this? The reluctant Pup is right amidst all of them — displaying, frothing, even barking. He wants in the game.

Isn't this the way football coaches handle their lackluster players? They don't leave them in the locker room. They make them sit on the bench (which is their chain gang) and agonize about the players getting the fun and the glory and the honor and the girls' cheers out on the field. The lackluster lad has nothing more for company than a scrawny team manager and a water bucket.

You bet the kid wants in the game — same as Pup.

The Walking Chain Gang

But there's more we can do. For example, let's train a gun-shy pup. To do this, we'll use the walking chain gang. Snap Pup in tandem with

The bird has been planted in a tuft of high grass. The handler of front dog (all-age status) has walked his dog into the scent cone. Two back-up helpers follow with two dogs in a chain gang—but each dog has his own check cord. A fourth helper can be the bird boy, who walks in and kicks the bird out, or the handler of the all-age dog will do the chore.

another dog that is not gun shy and a little advanced in training. Gun dog supply stores sell special devices to snap two dogs together, or you can just use two short check cords—one to each D-ring.

Have a bird boy walk the tandem afield—behind you. You have in hand an all-age, all-star performer—a real crackerjack. Now you come upon the tuft of grass. A second bird boy picks up the shackled bird, says *brrrrrrr-rrrrr* (but doesn't shoot) and lets the bird fly. To really accelerate the excitement, let the all-age dog break and give chase. This will excite Pup. I guarantee you he'll want in the game.

Keep doing this day after day.

One day, put the all-age dog in tandem and check-cord Pup, *alone*, into the bird's scent cone. When the bird is lofted by the second bird boy, let Pup break. Now we go to a homing pigeon with no hobble. Let the bird fly away with Pup in hot pursuit.

Once again, we do not fire a gun.

Now, how do we control a non-hobbled bird? Well, we plant him. I told you not to do it before, but now we must. To dizzy a bird, hold him head down and spin him around and around. Pick him up by his back in your right hand and pull his legs. If they relax, the bird's asleep. Lay him down with his head under the wing closest to earth. Okay? Incidentally, it'll take practice to dizzy a bird correctly.

On about the fifth or sixth day—all the while you're reading Pup, you know how he's feeling and what he wants all by the way he's acting—while Pup is chasing the fly-away bird and is far distant, *you fire the gun*. Should Pup ignore the retort, you've just scored a training breakthrough. If he stops and turns about to see what happened, you do nothing; in no way do you acknowledge anything happened. Should Pup actually give up his chase and come in, then put him back on the walking chain gang. Should he stop for a moment, then look where the bird went, you know you've got it made.

In future sessions, keep firing the gun when Pup is closer and on chase, until finally, you check-cord Pup into the bird's scent cone, walk up the cord, anchor Pup, let the bird boy *brrrrrr-rrrrrer* and throw a shackled bird, and this time the bird boy fires a training pistol. Still later, he fires a shotgun. And through it all Pup still wants to get the bird. Hooray, he's no longer gun shy.

And the fact of the matter is, neither is he cover shy, man shy, nor bird shy. You corrected all three of those faults, plus gun shyness, at the same time. And you did it by getting other dogs to train Pup.

You see, there is phenomenal communication constantly going on between dogs. I don't know how they do it, I just know they do it. Before I die there is nothing I'd love to learn more than just how dogs relate their feelings to one another. But I'll never get a breakthrough. I've tried so long to decipher their communications and have failed. I narrowed it down to scent discrimination or extra-sensory perception, but narrower I couldn't get it . . . and won't get it. All I know is, it exists and a dog trainer can use it by grouping dogs together in some training situations. We'll see it again when we go to the magic table where we teach retrieving.

Here, a bowline knot has been tied to strike the front edge of the dog's jaw. Note: the smooth part of knot is on top so the singed-off edge of nylon cord will not jab.

So Where Are We?

We've got Pup check-cording into the bird's scent cone, and we're holding him to stand steady to wing and shot. Or we got Pup on the chain gang, bolding him up. Or we have him as part of the walking chain gang, where we entice the lackluster Pup and bold up the gun-shy, man-shy, bird-shy, and cover-shy problem dog. Now we've got to get Pup into birds without holding him.

We do this with the bowline knot. Remember? We have a twenty- or twenty-two-foot check cord with a snap swivel attached to Pup's flat collar, and just at the outside terminus of his bottom jaw we have tied a bowline knot. When we flip the line, the knot bumps Pup under his chin. That upthrusts his head, which makes him rear back. Plus, we break Pup's concentration, and he does not step forward on whoa.

Well, that's what we're intentionally going to do now.

Now all gun dog training is point of contact (Pup's flat collar), repetition (repeating drills over and over), and association (our voice bouncing off Pup's ear drums with every drill until finally we let go the point of contact and rely on voice alone). That's when we have a trained dog.

Okay, remember, whoa has nothing to do with birds. It means for Pup to put all four feet flat and not move an eyelid. Nor do we say whoa around birds—until Pup no longer needs to hear it, when he's a sure whoaer. Then you say it not as a command, but as a support word. You're telling him he's doing his job right, you're proud of him, to look sharp, and be ready.

So we work Pup into the scent cone, but instead of walking down our rope, we walk about Pup in a great circle. There are several reasons for this. We never shoot birds standing over Pup. We always walk around him and go to front to keep the percussion from his ears: we don't want him suffering noise-induced hearing loss, nor do we want the noise to make him gun shy. Plus, by walking a great circle about Pup we can keep an eye on him. His shoulder muscles must move before Pup can lift a foot. We monitor these muscles. Should we see a muscle twitch, we twirl our check cord so the bowline knot strikes Pup on the bottom chin. This short-circuits his thinking and gets him pool-table solid.

The bowline knot also keeps Pup "head up." You know from divers and acrobats that as the head goes the body follows. The diver lowers her head before she leaps. On a back flip, she rears the head back. Same with Pup. We snap that bowline knot under his chin and up comes his head. This lowers his rump to keep him from breaking, but just as importantly it raises the head so he's "heads up" to watch the

Professional trainer Delmar Smith practices with a bowline knot attached to bench. He's got his timing right so that the knot slams into the dog's jaw just as the command is given to whoa.

birds fly away. That way he can relocate the scattered covey or watch where the deadfall came down.

Now there is this to know about flipping that bowline knot. If you flip late or early, you've spoiled the effect. Far as Pup's concerned, you've jolted him for nothing. So you must have split-second timing. Now let's introduce the command *whoa*. Outfit the bowline knot on the wrist and hand of a helpmate. Put a leather watch strap around your friend's wrist and attach the bowline knot. The tips of his fingers should be about the same length as the tip of Pup's jaw. Now flip the bowline knot and say, "Whoa." The knot should strike just as the command is heard. That's the association we spoke of above. Pup will associate the strike of the knot with the oral command. Then later, with no cord at all, you can be in front of Pup and when you flip your hand toward him he'll tighten up like a hoedowner's fiddle strings.

So that's our control: a check cord and a bowline knot. We keep drilling and kicking out the birds (ourselves) that we've planted, then having someone retrieve that bird while we go on to the next tuft of grass or mound of sticks. Or, we can just kick out homers that we've dizzied and let them fly home. For their holding is no longer so critical to us. Pup must also stop to flush, and it's good to have a bird come up before you're ready.

And there is this, too. Many field-trial judges penalize a dog for turning about and watching a bird down. They say it shows the dog is not steady to wing and shot. It also shows the judges are idiots. I'm not helping you train a field-trial dog (though your dog could probably place once he's a bona fide hunter); I'm teaching you how to build a gun dog. Part of a gun dog's responsibilities is to watch the bird down, either to go and point it again or fetch it up if it's been hit. How's he to do that if he doesn't watch? Judges are misnamed – and I've spoken of this before in other places. They should not be called judges. It gives them airs and a sense of invincibility. Instead, they should be called helpers, for their sole and express purpose out there is to help the handler and the dog show their best, if not at that meet, then at another one on down the line.

When you check-cord about Pup and reach the bird's hiding place, you either reach down and loft him up or give him a lift with the toe of your boot. Sometimes such pigeons will be so dazed (when dizzied) they walk about. Good. This duplicates what Pup will see on many game preserves where bobwhites don't have the snap to take to the airways and, instead, walk about on the ground or loft only to land on a tree limb. Besides, let the bird walk far enough and you can go to Pup and tap him on the back of his head, which is the sign to release him from point to relocate. Once again, he'll point the bird. You just got two points out of one bird, and that's great.

Use homing pigeons for these drills and they'll be waiting in their coop when you get home. I've never had a bird die in training except when chewed by a hard-mouth dog or killed as part of a drill. All the rest lived to a ripe old age and raised many squabs for the training field.

But don't buy homers and think they'll home to your coop. They won't. They'll go to the coop from whence they were purchased. Their offspring, however, will know your coop as their home, and that's where they'll fly each time they're released.

Now, there are at least two more things we need to discuss.

Always stop Pup at the first hint he's struck a scent cone. Never let him barge on in, catwalk, creep, what have you. Make sure he's stopped when he's scented game. If not, Pup will crowd wild birds and flush them up. It just stands to reason domesticated birds are going to sit tighter and hold longer than their wild cousins. That's why some people say they'll never train on pen-raised birds. The dogs flush wild birds in the field. But bosh to this. If you stop the dog at the edge of the bird's scent cone, he'll never crowd them and never push them to flight.

Another thing to discuss is honor.

While check-cording, this pointer pup has broken honor. Professional trainer Randy Patterson picks Pup up and carries him to spot he vacated.

Honoring Another Dog's Work

There are two ways a dog stands to wing and shot. One is to point the covey, or the single, and stand there. The other is to honor. The honoring dog is a bracemate that has not found the birds. Thus, his obligation is to honor the dog who has. The pointing dog scents the game and points, the honoring dog sees the pointer and honors on sight. Both dogs whoa — one because of scent, the other because of sight.

The way we teach honor is identical to the way we bring a bird dog to game. We check-cord both dogs into the scent cone, and the first dog pointing has the right-of-way. The other dog cannot encroach nor in any way interfere. So the moment the lead dog points, the handler of the honoring dog holds fast the check cord, comes down it hand over hand, and kneels beside the honoring dog just as though he were pointing game.

There is this, though. Should the honoring dog be outside the scent cone, the handler has the option of picking the dog up and carrying him to where he'll get a snootful. The point being, an honoring dog can never move a foot on honor. That's why you carry him — you never heel him forward, for example.

Then the bird boy makes his great arc about the pointing dog, reaches down and picks up the hobbled bird, makes a great display, lofts the bird, and fires (or does not fire) a blank training pistol. Both dogs watch the bird dance and the fly away. Both dogs go berserk.

Later you'll have both dogs running in front of you while trailing a check cord. When the lead dog makes point, the handler of the honoring dog rushes forward and stands beside the trailing check cord. He'll leave it free, place a boot sole on it, or actually take it to hand — it all depends on what he knows about his pupil. Just how steady he figures the honoring dog really is.

Should a dog on check cord, or running free, ever break honor and race toward the pointing dog, the handler is to run and catch him and pick him up and tell him exactly what he thinks of him and bring him back and place him in the exact spot he vacated when he broke honor. All dogs are extremely place-oriented. The errant pooch will know. But there is this. As you run forward to get the breaking honor dog, don't say anything that will put the lead dog off his game. Be silent. Tell the dog what you think of him in a grating whisper. Don't interfere with the working dog.

Later, when both dogs are finished, you can do what you want. The lead dog will know he's not at error, he'll not go off game because you're raising hell with the honor dog that broke.

Remember, dogs can be very bright. But you've got to give them the time to become bright. It doesn't happen in the litter box. It comes about through months afield with you – and tons of birds. Plus dogs learn the game. They know what's going on. That dog who broke, he knows he did wrong – and so does his pointing bracemate. No one's going to get confused after they've got some age on them.

Kenneling

There is no particular time to teach a dog to kennel, but more than likely it will come up early in life. For good potty training, the dog must sleep in a kennel crate all night in your bedroom. You'll have to tell him to kennel as you put him in there.

Then you'll need to tell him to kennel when you're putting him in a kennel run, into a pickup truck, the rear end of a station wagon, the door to a motel room, and so on.

Paramount to kenneling is getting twice your money's worth. This means Pup should usually be asked to kennel at some elevation higher than he's standing. For example, his dog house (should he have one outdoors) should be two feet from the ground so he is constantly leaping up and down all day long. This will build up those pelvic drive muscles needed for thrust in a bird field.

Also, akin to teaching Pup to kennel is teaching him to jump. Now that's usually simple enough. But we can aid it along. Even a young Pup can have a two-by-eight-inch board placed in a doorway so he must jump over it to get from room to room. On advanced Pups, I like to put them in a baby pen and leave them. They'll learn to jump out to be near you. Then there's no chore to get them to jump to a wagon's tailgate, nor up and over a fence. For leaping fences will be a part of the hunt.

So, now we've taken Pup through the basics. Honest, folks, he is already a better performer, and he's already had more effective training, than one dog out of a thousand. And we hardly did a thing, did we? It's just that when you're acting right, everything naturally falls in place. But most bird dogs will have a problem, and to them we'll now turn.

5

Bird Dog Problems

YOU'LL BE SURPRISED how many bird dog problems we've already addressed and solved. But let's get to our list. I'll refer you to key words in the index for further study, or I'll give a brief summation of what we did to overcome some particular problem.

Heel
We taught heel with the power bar. See *power bar* in the index.

Sit
Most bird dog men don't want their dogs to sit. It too closely approximates a dog dropping on point—which is the way all bird dogs hunted in the beginning. Before the invention of gunpowder, birds were netted. The bird dog would locate the bird, then drop so the net could be thrown over his head. Even today, some bird dogs slink to point and relocation. They are just naturally bred and trained to stay low.

So we do not teach the bird dog to sit, but to stand. This is done by pumping up. You know the sequence. A guy pops you on the shoulder and knocks you sideways. He pops you again and you brace. He pops you a third time and you lean into the blow. That's how we pump Pup

This alert gun dog is no blinker. He lifted chukar on a stop to flush, the handler fired and hit, and now the dog waits handler's instructions for fetch.

up. Incidentally, you'll sometimes see Pup "sitting" on the whoa post, so you'll need to know the antidote. Make a bridge of your non-gun hand, extending the thumb and the little finger. Place this bridge over the dog's lower backbone just before his hips. Start pumping. The dog will inflate like a balloon.

Stay
Stay is the same as whoa for the bird dog man. See *whoa* in the index.

Come
We taught come (or *here*, as it is preferred by some gun dog men) with the power bar. See *power bar* in the index.

Hie On
Hie on is an English term telling the dog to get hunting. In America, the handler is just as apt to say, "All right," and give the dog a lifting and launching thrust with the back of his collar. Or he merely taps the dog behind the head to indicate he should relocate. (This is a shortened version of a complete cast to extend.)

Hie on is an easy command to instill, for the average bird dog wants to get on with it from the beginning. However, it can be heightened when the dog breaks (such as when we were curing gun shyness). As the dog leaves, the handler yells, "All right," and he'll be gone.

Blinking

Pup will usually blink a bird because he's bird shy or he's just not a bird dog. Test him. Plant a bird. Know exactly where the bird is, then check-cord Pup into the scent cone. If he shows he's scented the bird but has no interest, then work him into the bird until the bird launches. If Pup makes no effort either to leap and trap the bird or to chase after it, you've got a bona fide blinker.

And a bona fide blinker is a dog that, though he's located a bird, will let on he hasn't and pass it on by, going on another fruitless hunt — never, ever getting a bird to sit for wing and shot.

Now, we've already handled part of this problem by making Pup agonize on the chain gang and endure the walking chain gang. This should have birdied him up to where he will no longer blink a bird. But what if he persists?

Take Pup hunting with another dog: keep both dogs on separate check cords. Have the bird flushed and shoot to kill. Then, give the bird to Pup to eat. If he refuses it — won't have anything to do with it — we'll have to go yet one more step.

Denying Pup all other food, put him in a kennel run with twelve bobwhite quail. Pup will now chase the birds down, kill them, and eat — or go hungry. If you see he's just going to starve himself to death, then you'll need to discard him. Not all dogs are curable of all problems.

But more than likely, before Pup will actually see his ribs stick together, he'll start killing and eating live quail. Now once more take him to field with the other dog (remember, Pup is still not being fed) and offer Pup the bird the other dog pointed and you shot. If Pup eats, then you're on your way. Continue to give Pup the birds you shoot over him — for now the other dog is retired. Of course, you must one day cure Pup of eating birds, but this is easily done with the magic table when teaching retrieve.

Now is as good a time as any to post a truth midst all gun dog training. When you solve one problem, usually you create another. It's just built into the process. That's the problem with problems. They can go and on, from one drill to another, until sometimes you have to make the decision whether or not the dog is worth salvaging.

Pointing Unproductives

Akin to blinking a bird is to point an unproductive. Pup's given every sign the bird is there, but the hunter cannot lift it. Once again, over-look one incident, be leery of a second, and get mighty concerned if there's a third.

There may be several things happening. It might be a day where scenting conditions are so poor Pup couldn't find his feed pan. Other than that, it may be a windy day and the birds are skittish. Or, it could be raining and they don't want to fly, so they're running. Tell Pup to relocate, and see if he produces feather.

Maybe Pup's goofing off, pointing nothing just to keep from working, or putting you off your game because of a grudge he holds for you. Yes, dogs can be that bright, and brighter.

Or it could be Pup's bird shy, but wants to please. He'll go through the motions to gain your goodwill, but he'll never face a bird.

Well, we solve all this many ways. We put Pup on the chain gang, we make him participate in the walking chain gang, or we put him through the poultry program described under blinking. Pup has to kill birds to eat.

Now, you're not always going to understand solutions I pose to problems presented. But here's a case where Pup should also be put on the magic table and taught to retrieve. (See chapter 6). The table is magic for many reasons. It makes meek Pups stick their chests out; it makes bullheaded Pups let their milk down; it makes fighters lower their dukes. It's just a great doganizer . . . like our word humanizer. It makes the dog want to be a part of the man/dog family. And it also makes Pup get along better with other dogs. But what it does most is instill bird love in Pup, which can manifest itself by Pup no longer leading you to unproductives.

Bolting

The bolter can be one of many things. He can be zany and runs amuck for the sheer joy of it; he may be a self-hunter and wants the whole bird game to himself; or he just has so much vinegar there's not a vista far enough for him to reach.

Bolting can be one of the worst problems in dogdom to solve.

We've all seen a bolter. Or rather, we haven't seen him. We released him to hunt, and he was gone for the day, the week, the month. I've known them to be gone for years.

As bird populations become scant, this is a problem we'll see more and more in the future. Pup wants to hunt and he's running to find game. Fact is, he's going too damned fast. He smells only on the intake, and in a quarter of a mile he's so hot he can't smell at all—and this just further aggravates our predicament.

There is only one cure. Seed the bird field with as many birds as you can physically afford and put out. Now Pup's got so many birds before him he must stop to honor: that is, he must point. Use homers so you don't lose a bird. Keep doing it. Get Pup to thinking there's game every thirty feet, and he'll give up his marathons.

Or, and this is interesting, load a saddle bag with birds and hang the bag on your belt or over your shoulder. When Pup's out a ways, reach in the bag, give a whoop to get Pup looking at you, and throw a bird. This will get him running back to you. Later, just drop the bird out so it sets; when you whoop and Pup runs to investigate, he'll flush the bird himself.

The thing is, this is a dog that can never be lied to. You must produce birds, tons of birds, and he must be in constant bird contact. Then and only then will he give up his forward race. And he must learn to trust you. When you indicate birds, they have to be there. Let's say the bird you dropped when you said whoop walked away. Well, be ready to drop another. Pup must always prove successful on his back cast.

There are other ways to control Pup's forward race. Gun dog supply stores sell rubber balls hung on cords that you attach to Pup's collar. Or you can hang a cut-open inner tube (or a gunny sack) like an apron from his collar and make him run hobbled. But this is not curing the problem; this is just hindering the offender until he can be free to take off again.

Possibly the best hobble I've ever known of is a thirty-, sixty-, or ninety-foot section of garden hose attached to Pup's collar. Dragging that around a while will shorten his race and take the bolt out of him. But nothing succeeds like birds.

So there's really only one way to get a bolter in pocket, and that's to plant so many birds he's got to stop and honor them. You may just make a bird dog of him – and you may not.

I admit I've designed this book for the foot hunter. But the man on horseback does have advantages. For one thing, a bolter, to a man on foot, could well be a dog with an extended race to a man on horseback – as long as the dog produces game. But the reason I bring up the horse is this. Gun dog horses become very savvy; they know the game as well as the dog. And some horses have been trained to run down the bolter and slap an oversized horseshoe on the trailing check cord. The dog goes tail over teacup and comes up dazed, no longer invincible. He worries about taking off again and hunts closer.

Cutting Back

A dog that loops each cast till he ends up back at the man who launched him is a backtracker. Such a looping dog is uncertain of what lies to front. He also can be shy or he's not birdy. Nothing could bold him up like the magic table to teach retrieve. Plus we've got a handful of other alternatives. Like the bolter, he can run in a seeded field. He can't help but find birds. Now there's no need for him to come back: the birds shortstop him.

Or he can agonize on the chain gang or be a part of the walking chain gang. He also can be put on the poultry program where he must eat birds to live. I'd be prone to say this dog was never Happy Timed. He didn't learn the terrain, the game, or the bird. His world did not disappear. Remember? A dog must be so at home in the wild his world disappears. Then he only has birds to fill his mind.

Another trick with the looping dog is to sing a constant song. Let the dog know where you are. How does the song go? Well it's not actually a song, it's just a series of *HALLLLLOOOOOOOS* distinctive to each handler. The dog always knows where the man is so if there is some timidity involved he can stay to front, knowing he's not lost. One old-time handler I knew tackled looping this way: whenever he saw such a dog coming back to him, he'd take his jackknife and cut a bush with lots of leaves. Then he'd run at the dog, screaming, brandishing the foliage, driving the dog back to field. It worked. At the same time, the man held his hat aloft and "threw" it at the dog. That is, the hat was brought forward with a throwing motion but never released. Later still, the man could see the dog returning and turn him back on his forward race by producing the hat.

Other handlers have done just the opposite. When they see the dog returning, they completely ignore him: even when he's standing to side. Finally, the dog will cast out on his own.

In the end, there is a figure-eight collar device that works as follows. You collar the errant pooch to a dog that never comes in and let them both go. But one thing you must watch. You can have one heck of a dog fight – and it's serious. These dogs are eyeball to eyeball and mouth to mouth. I've also had dogs get so nervous that the problem dog upchucked almost immediately after being collared.

As for me, I think all this can be solved with the walking chain gang and the magic table. Anyway, that's the way I've solved it, and if it works for me it sure should work for you.

Ranging Too Far

This Pup's not a bolter; he just hunts too far out, way beyond gun range. It's not really a problem so long as he holds his point. But it is a problem in brushy country where you spend the day hunting your dog instead of birds.

Here's what you do. Like the bolter, you run him in a seeded field. All the birds are planted, so why run to the next county? Or you call out *whoop*, get the dog's attention, and throw out a bird from your saddle bag.

But most of all you return to check-cording: teaching Pup to quarter on voice and hand signals. Then, when you cry "Ho" and Pup's far to field, he spins around to see what you want and you give him a right- or left-hand cast. That way, you've got him running laterally in the field and stopping his forward drive. Which is to say, you've got Pup hunting for you, and that's what we all want.

Bush Pointing

A bush pointer is a dog that's running a milk route on you. You've trained him so many times in this field he naturally knows where he's found birds and he goes there; not finding anyone home, he automatically points. The only way to handle this dog is to walk out the field beforehand — making sure no wild birds have moved in — and then when Pup bush points you ignore him, walking on by. He'll quit the false point and race to catch up and pass you. Enough times and he'll quit bush pointing altogether.

Or better yet, change fields. In this regard, it's necessary you know training grounds are hard to find. And most people go about it with so little tact. They approach a farmer or his wife and ask if they can train dogs on their property. They supply no credentials, but more importantly, they supply no aid-in-kind.

I once wrote a poem about it. I'm not saying it's a good poem, but I am saying it's a good thought. It went something like this:

I'm worth their visit but twice a year:
    In the spring for my fish,
    In the fall for my deer.
They cheer me on sayin', "How do things go?"
    But they're askin' for knowledge
    They don't want to know.
They're being polite till they can get on
    To trompin' my forest,
    Or stalkin' my pond.
For fret I should on price of crops,
    They'll worry some, sayin'
    "Sure hope they don't drop."

But drop clear out, I'll not get their pity.
    The problems that count —
    They're left in the city.
Or have snow drifted clean over by gables,
    I'll dig out alone,
    Good as I'm able.
Or come a flood and I'm baggin' sand,
    I'll not be expectin'
    A helpin' hand.
Or mendin' fence or thrashin' grain —
    I'm out of their thoughts,
    This keeper of game.
This keeper of game who'd be thrown out
    If into the city
    I'd come with a shout
Of "Howdy do," and enter their lives,
    Walk through their homes
    And ask of their wives,
"Your husband in? We've come to play,
    To idle about,
    To spend our day.
First croquet, then bar-b-cue.
    A dip in your pool
    And when that's through,
We'll be movin' on to another place . . .
    His name I forget
    But never a face!"
So, seen this way I hope it's plain
    A farmer's a farmer,
    Not a *keeper of game.*
And you who want his land for play,
    You'd do well
    To go some day
With guns and rods and all you love
    Left in the city —
    Just bring gloves.

Trailing

Tug died with the last rose of summer. He ate his evening meal, walked across the living room rug, and dropped dead. Just like he'd been shot in the brain. I heard him fall, he hit that hard. And I ran to him only to yell back to my wife, "Tug is dead." It was incredible. It was impossible.

Not only for Mom and me, but for the dogs who live in the house and shared Tug's eleven-year life.

There are a lot of dead dog stories. They always get to you. The loss, the sadness. The fact of their going leaves a great vacancy; the fact of their going foretells our own fate. The writer deals in touch relics, memory pictures. He or she tells of the vacancy beneath the bed, the empty feed bowl, the left-behind collar. And we need some of that. For a while, at least, it makes us protective of our other pets. It makes us ponder our own mortality.

But there's more to it than that.

A dead dog can tell us of our own ignorance. Our own neglect.

I look into the vacant backyard where Tug used to search for field mice – he was a terrier and this was his genetic mission – and can see him hiking a leg on a tomato plant. I think of all the times he came to me and I rejected him. He was so hard to love. As a terrier he had claws like a four-toothed grubbing hoe. (*Terrier* comes from Latin and means earth: a dog that digs in the earth.) And Tug was antsy. So any time he leaped into my lap so I could rub his ears, he would dig. But the claws would hurt, and I would push him away.

Yet that being antsy was his vitality. And that vitality made him the spark plug of the house. Kind of like a cheerleader. Now the dogs left behind are listless and forlorn. They have no one to take them hunting, to sustain the barking at the jet's sonic boom, to attack the garbage truck, or to lead everyone out after the ten o'clock news and tinkle.

And though I recognized and granted his leadership, still I failed to see his exact position in the pack's pecking order. I figured an old female was the hammer. She'd snap and Tug would sulk away, gulping with dry tongue, looking back with too much white in his eyes. But she was just protecting her own comforts and her own space. When it came time to do something, she turned the reins over to Tug.

So this dead dog story is written not to twang your heart strings, but instead to have you look at your own dog family. To have you better understand the furry world you took in for bed and board.

Oh, there's no way I could analyze your household. That's not the point. You're too far away and there are too many variables. But my emphasis is for you to look.

It matters not if the dog you own is bedecked with jeweled collar and pampered with silk pillows. That dog differs not one iota from the mud-splattered coon hound brawling through a timber tangle to come home and sleep in an oil drum. Every living creature has a unique relationship with every other and that includes man or dog. And to train a dog, to control him to do that thing you seek, you're better off if you understand these interrelationships.

Take bird dogs. There are three very bad, nigh on impossible, faults to cure. They are gun shyness, chasing deer, and trailing. The first two faults can be totally unique to the individual dog; they can exist independent of his relationship to other dogs. But trailing—that's a different story.

A trailer is a dog that won't self-hunt. Instead, he duplicates the running of a bracemate. Such a dog is not hunting, he is merely running. As a result, though you put two dogs down to cover twice as much territory, you end up with two dogs hunting the same ground in tandem—or more precisely, one dog hunting and the other dog tagging along.

There are two types of trailers. The first type is easy to spot; he simply gets behind his bracemate and follows him wherever he goes. The second type—the head trailer—is much harder to identify. He's a master of disguise. He stays in front, but with the corner of an eye he's continually checking back at his bracemate, and he turns whichever way the rear dog goes.

So how do you break a dog of trailing? Most times you don't. But here's what we try.

Most pros will put an electronic collar on the trailing dog and shock him every time he nears the lead dog or every time he turns the same direction as the lead dog. Yet, I have seen trailing dogs in shock collars—with the trainer giving full power—just grit their teeth; their bodies go one way, but their heads angle back toward the lead dog.

I've known other dog trainers who say you should hunt the trailing dog with two other dogs. He can't follow both. But they miss the point. Here's where we get to this power of interrelationships. Maybe the trailer will follow only one dog. Probably his mother, or an older, more seasoned dog that he was raised with. Consequently, he'll follow only this dog and ignore the other runner. The trailer lacks self-initiative and gives over his options to another. He feels secure only in imitating.

Such a dog must be bolded up. We do many things in dog training that make no sense to the layman. You cannot love a dog to performance. The dog doing a bad job takes such acts of love as confirmation he's doing right. No, the bad dog must be handled with a firm hand. I don't mean a brutal hand. I mean a thoughtful, gentle, but firm hand. After all, don't we call dog trainers handlers?

Well, what bolds a dog up? Again the layman will be confused with what I suggest. The dog needs to be put on a chain gang (see *chain gang* in the index). Let me repeat what I said up front. A chain gang is

Handler check-cords a high-flying pointer to a bird field planted with hobbled pigeons. Gunner lags behind. Each dog on the chain gang must agonize the working dog's good fortune as each bird lofts, is shot, and is brought to hand. Now the chain gang has its fire up.

like a trotline you use to catch catfish. It's a long chain secured at both ends with a series of drop chains attached. All the dogs are placed on this chain, not only to learn to give to the lead, but to fire them up.

Put all the dogs on one chain gang and work the other dogs on live birds before them. The submissive dog may get jerked around on that chain for two weeks with no effect. He may insist on looking the other way: away from the bird field. He may sulk and dig deep holes and sink himself beneath earth to confirm his misery. But that dog must stay on that chain. For, miracle of miracles, there'll come a day he pops out of his blue funk. There'll come a day he's leaping and barking and begging to be let into the game. Now we no longer have a submissive dog; we now have one asserting his own free will—telling us he wants to do something on his own. Without laying a hand on the dog, we have bolded him up. That's the best of all gun dog training, letting other dogs do it.

Of course, you can speed this along. Every training session you can fly a bird right over the wallflower. Or better yet, give him a dead bird to eat. That's right, this won't make the dog hard mouthed, or make him a bird eater. But it will sure show him what you want him to hunt, and it will prove to him the value of doing it. In this regard, some pros have a "poultry program." Here, the faulted dog is fed minimum rations, and he starts to look for the dead bird to fill his tummy. Pros undertake this program because they know a dog won't perform for you without a reason. You make the reason the dead bird, since the treat you give is the very thing you want the dog to hunt.

When you release the tied-up, former trailer, he knows the value of birds; he has been shown by you where such birds are to be found in likely cover; and he takes off on the cast to get him one. Later, it's your job to break him over to hunt for you instead of for himself. But that's dog training. It's always links in a chain. You get one link secure, then you fit the second link, and on and on. But inevitably, the master link in the chain is the bird: *I know of no gun dog problem that can't be solved with a bird.*

That's why the suggestion that you just hunt the trailer alone has little merit. Such a dog might not even cast from your side.

But there's another solution that has worked. I once had a liver-and white-pointer bitch that resembled the character in the old joke about the fighting dog. You remember, the guy cut the alligator's tail off and painted him yellow. Ol' Yeller could whip any dog in town.

Well, Anny (that was her misgiven name, it should have been Tornado, or something equally devastating) would broach no interference with her bird work. She'd take a stand on a bird with all the blocky purchase of an upright Coke machine. You couldn't drag her off a point with a power take off.

All I had to do was release the trailer to hunt with Anny. If she didn't get tired of his tailing her, she mighty sure got tired of it when the trailer tried to close in on honor or even steal a point. That's when Anny would leave her point – and the only time – to damn near kill the encroacher. She would give that dog such a thrashing that he'd never again want anything to do with her. When let loose together, the reformed trailer would now jump sideways to hunt the adjacent country.

There are lots of ways to skin a cat, they say, or to train a dog, and you have to use your ingenuity to come up with the program that will help you best. And to do that you must consider the interrelationship of the animals you're working with – as well as their relationship to you.

What of the dog that wilts with one handler, but becomes a stellar performer with another? Here's the case of the dog being okay, but his relationship with his trainer being at fault.

So be sensitive, be observant, be patient. Think things through and then rethink them again. Don't get so mechanical in your relationships with your dogs that you really don't see them, or just go through routine without actually tailoring a program to the individual dog. I became so accustomed to my house pack that I frankly never saw them—though I thought I did. Tug proved that. And for that I surely wish him lots of nummy-nummy, green fields to run in, and a place to sleep under God's bed.

Gun Shyness

That chunk of chain you've got staked under the shade trees so Pup won't get too hot—well, leave it there. That chain will also help us cure the bird-shy, gun-shy, man-shy, and cover-shy dog.

But first let's make sure what we're talking about. Through selective breeding and culling, the average gun dog is not gun shy. Consequently, the only way he can become shy is through an accident afield. I'll give you an example. Pup's on point. As the handler brushes past, he takes a thorn bush with him that releases to snap back and slap Pup in the face just as the bird flushes and the gun goes off. Now we've got a gun-shy, bird-shy, man-shy, cover-shy Pup, and it all came about in one second. But this is an accident. We can cure accidents. They're man-made. But what if the accident is God-made?

What I speak of here is the true gun-shy dog that comes from the womb a trembling mess. He leaps at the sound of thunder, a slammed door, a dropped shoe—he's so frightened of his world and so uncertain of himself he won't even eat if you put his food bowl in a different place. Now this dog was wired wrong in the womb, and there is nothing we can do to cure him.

So we'll concentrate only on accident-shy dogs, okay?

What we must do is bold the errant pooch up—and thus, once again, we use the chain gang. And we use it exactly as we used it to cure the trailer. In other words, what we're doing is positioning Pup so he'll be trained by other dogs. There is no other technique in dog training so effective. For you must know that nothing bad can ever happen to a dog that he can associate with man. If he's to be put in stress, then let him work it out with others of his own kind. Never a man. And by the same token, you should know that if something does go wrong, Pup will associate the pain or the displeasure with the place it occurred. Pup should never be taken to that spot again.

Okay, as an amateur you're hard-pressed to find all those dogs to make that chain gang shake, rattle, and roll. So you must do one of three things: join a gun dog club and go train with others of like mind; offer your assistance to a professional dog trainer who will help you for the work you do for him; or make friends with a guy who has several dogs and (as the pro) needs someone to help him train. In return, he'll work your dog into his string. I've done all three, plus, I've gathered up the neighborhood pack and snapped them on the chain gang—everything from Pomeranians to pit bulls.

Once again, you work all-age dogs on live birds in front of Pup and make him eventually agonize to get into the game. But let's say you just can't find the dogs to help you. Okay, then let's go to the walking chain gang (which is where we were headed anyway).

What we have here is a golden triangle: three dogs. We need one all-age dog (sure and steady) and another partially broke dog to couple with Pup. And when I say couple, that's exactly what I mean. You can either walk Pup and his bracemate on two ropes or you can use one rope with a "power take off." (This is a Y-shaped device sold at gun dog supply stores. Made of leather, chain, or nylon, you clip each dog to one arm of the Y.)

I've said before there's not a problem with dogs that can't be solved with birds. What I might not have emphasized is I'm talking about lots of birds. And the bird of choice is the common barnyard pigeon. Choose a bird field of mowed grass in which you've left tufts of high grass or have stacked brush up to form a haven for the planted bird. Now you plant birds by dizzying them. (You could work the birds out of catapult launchers, but given the number of birds we need, you'd have to buy a lot of launchers, and that would prove expensive.)

To dizzy a bird, take the pigeon and tuck his head under one wing. Keep that wing up and hold it in your hand, which you rotate like you were turning an old ice cream churn. When the bird's released, place him on the ground with the head-wing down. You can tell if the bird's relaxed by stretching his legs. If they stay elongated with no contraction, then the bird is sufficiently dizzied.

Okay, plant all the birds you've got.

Now, work the all-age dog into the scent cone of each bird, whoa him, walk around him, kick out the planted bird—*but don't fire a gun.* Never fire. Let the golden triangle of bird dogs watch the launched bird fly away. Now go to the next planted bird. Tour the field. Also, keep watching the gun-shy dog. He'll tell you by his actions what progress he's making.

Remember, you can't train a dog unless you can read him. And a dog is constantly sending you messages. But you may not catch them, for the messages, to you, are a foreign language. Well, there's no way around it, you spend enough years in the field and you'll start to see and decode the signs. In the beginning of all this, the gun-shy dog will either sulk and be dragged along or he'll flat go zany. If he goes berserk, he'll leap, squeal, squirm, flip, and dodge. Just have the helper keep a tight rope on the tandem and keep up.

Later, you'll begin to see the gun-shy dog settling. He'll be more attentive to the working dog, he'll watch you, plus he'll be sensing and responding to the co-dog hooked in tandem. What's more, he'll become entranced with the fly-away bird.

After you've gone afield several days with no gun—go several more.

Now you put the all-age dog in tandem with Pup and release the nearly broke dog to work the birds. Repeat the sequence. Remember, *don't fire the gun.* Create a lot of hoopla, dance about, shout, kick the bird up with great flair. Point the gun, but don't shoot it. Let the bird fly away so three dogs have a long, lingering look—except the working dog: he's permitted to give full chase if he wants to.

Eventually, you release the gun-shy dog to work while the all-age dog and the partially broke dog work in brace. Once again, you repeat the sequence. Lots of hoopla, kick out the bird, and let Pup break to give chase.

As always you continue to read Pup, to note his aggressiveness, his boldness, his birdiness. When you finally feel his enthusiasm for birds is so great it'll overcome anything, it's time to fire the gun: but only while Pup is far distant and in full chase.

If Pup does not stop his chase, turn around, hesitate, or in any way honor the retort of the gun, you've just scored a gun dog training breakthrough.

Do this many more days. Always, dog training takes at least twice as long as you feel it does, or it should. That's the law of the game. The unbreakable law.

Eventually, you'll whoa the (once) gun-shy dog, walk about him in a great circle, kick out the bird, and fire the gun—all right in front of Pup. Now the dog stands to shot and wing (after you've taught him whoa with the whoa post or the bowline knot), and you've salvaged a dog for the bird field.

As you work with the gun, give Pup the whole bird to eat. For several weeks thereafter, always let him have the head of the dead bird. No need concerning yourself with Pup becoming a bird eater or hard mouth: we'll correct that on the magic table.

Now let's back up.

I've written countless places that I do not know how dogs communicate: but they do. Which means all during our training procedure the gun-shy dog has been in constant communication with his bracemate, the all-age dog up front, you, the bird, the sky, the wind, the soil, and the gut-burning reality of his own fright. And all other dogs have been in identical communication with the gun-shy dog. They know how he feels. And this is important: I've had more than one gun-shy dog brought to me for cure and learned the handler was gun shy. The dog was cuing off the man. Same with bolting. The pheasant runs, the man lets the dog give chase; then to stay within gun range, the man starts running. Now we have a bolting man.

So we don't know how dogs communicate, and maybe we never will. But we do know such communication is constantly going on, so we honor this by being as sensitive as we can. You'll recall my mentioning Mike Gould and his old performer, the Labrador, Web. Mike has what he calls an invisible rubber band. You get this with long relationships—not with pups. It takes years to develop. That was the case with Dan Patch, the greatest pacing horse that ever lived. He never lost a race. A man named Marion Savage was Dan's final owner, and Marion's son, Harold, once said, "There was something uncanny, almost supernatural, about their relationship from the moment they met until the end." It's imponderable to note the mighty trotter and his owner passed away thirty-two hours apart.

And so it's been with dogs I've owned. I had an English border collie named Banjo; he could be a quarter mile to field, but if I took three steps to my right (or to my left) that dog—which was running away from me and couldn't really see what I was doing—would suddenly swerve and go the direction I was stepping. Again, the invisible rubber band.

Well, with the golden triangle of dogs you've got invisible rubber bands going in every direction. And they're all beneficial. I admit, some of my advice may look too simple to be effective. Well, don't question what I say, just do it. It works. And be ever vigilant to whatever sign you think you can pick up from any one or all three of the dogs. The result will be breaking a gun-shy dog to the gun. Friends, that—along with curing bolting and trailing—is the toughest thing to get done in dogdom.

Running Trash

Running trash is a bird dog term meaning the dog pursues nongame. Usually such a dog is bred close to carnal instincts and is just fascinated with meat on the hoof. Such dogs chase poultry, cattle, rabbits, skunks, coon, box turtles (if you can call that a chase), and especially deer. Now, bird dogs are big in Dixie, and that's where deer presently

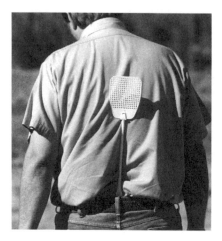

Chesapeake Bay retriever handler Butch Goodwin secrets a white flyswatter behind his back and goes to work. He has here the most effective training device ever conceived—except the check cord or the leather collar.

average forty bushels to the acre. There are so many deer in the South they are changing the habitat by eating certain species of shrub and trees extinct. So, you mention the one most prominent problem in the most-populated bird dog country in the world, and the answer will come, "Chasing deer."

The traditional way to take dogs off deer is to equip them with an electronic collar that emits a shock when a remote control is actuated. The dog gets electrocuted in the neck just when (the theory goes) the dog nears the deer. Then, *Eureka!* The dog thinks the deer did it and gives up chasing them forever. Hog wash. A deer is a fleet animal that lives in heavy brush. How, tell me, are you going to know when the dog is close to the deer when you can't see either dog or deer? And if you can't see the dog, you can't shock him. Not if you're a dog trainer. So the system is stupid. But America loves gimmicks. A little while ago I was grayling fishing on a small pond in the Arizona White Mountains. Rome has water fountains larger than this pond. And a guy yells over at me, "My fish detector is picking up all kinds of fish sign." Why doesn't he also use it in his aquarium to know where they're hiding? God, is there nothing left in nature that we can't detect, chase down, and/or destroy with a machine? That's why I love canoeing and sailboat fishing. It's just me and the elements, just me and nature, going with the whims of the wind, trusting to my own seasoned judgment where the fish are biting and what they want to eat. Man and his infernal damned machines. Such men never marry Mother Nature, they just rape her and dump her. Such men just don't have much fertilizer in their plots. They're brain-dead and kept alive by a machine.

But back to training dogs.

I admit deer are a horrible problem for the bird dog man. Almost an insurmountable problem. But there is a way I try to take dogs off deer. Find out where deer are feeding, even bait them, then check-cord your dog into their scent. When the dog honors the hot blood of the chase, chastise him severely. You see, the most severe torture instrument ever perfected for a man to use on a dog (and the only one I use when I insist on getting my point across) is a white plastic fly-swatter. Ideally it should have been started on a seven-week-old pup to teach house training. But still, I've converted many a tough old-timer to the flyswatter. Just swat him across the butt with that swatter and tell him in no uncertain terms he is not going to chase deer. He is not even going to honor the fact they passed that way.

Horse, man, or dog—when you've taken their feet away from them, they're yours. So if Pup won't give you proper respect for your flyswatter in the beginning, then physically pick him up by grabbing the fur on each side of his neck and hold the dog directly in front of your face while you tell him what you think.

Let the dog smell your rage, sense your heat, be blasted with the volume. Let him know this is mighty damned serious and you're not going to put up with it. Then put him down and show him the fly-swatter. For that will be your point of association when Pup's a quarter mile away. Just yell him down and hold that swatter high. His light will go on.

If Pup shows your message is falling on deaf ears, then suddenly drop him to earth and immediately straddle him. Now, hold him on his back and yell right up his nose. Since you're in the position of riding a horse, make the flyswatter your riding crop and let him have it across his hip—all the while you're yelling.

And once again, you must know how to read your dog. You will soon learn when he's making game on deer. You'll see all the signs; the nose goes down, the hackles rise, the head abruptly comes up, and *zoooooom*, he's off. Well, short circuit all this. When you see the first telltale signs, yell "No." But I admit, the worst scenario is when Pup unwittingly jumps a deer from its bed. Now you've really got a mess. For the deer is going to run. And *Whooppee*, Pup takes off. Well, when you finally run Pup down, go through all the steps above. But don't call Pup to you to punish him. For in his mind that's what he did wrong— he came to you. No. Catch him in pursuit, and flyswatter him good.

Now, there's no end to man's folly. I'll tell you a true story. There were two men who were co-owners of a deer-chasing fool. This dog would rather chase deer than eat. So the two men got their heads together and decided what they needed to do was buy the meanest

The best introduction to water for a gang of pups is the farm pond on a hot summer day. Second best is to toss the lot of them to raging flood waters where they must turn and swim into the current to await delayed-thrown dummies. In the top photo, pups prep for water entry. They crash through brittle brush to once again show their boldness, and then paddle like hell upcurrent, awaiting arrival of the late-thrown decoys. This is Roaring Fork, which passes Mike Gould's training grounds at Carbondale, Colorado.

billy goat on earth. To their minds, there'd be a lot of transfer between a goat and a deer. And if they could make that dog disgusted with that goat, then he'd stay off deer forever.

So they shopped and shopped until they found just what they wanted: a big, mangy-looking, old billy with gigantic horns and a lean form who looked mighty hungry – and looked mighty mean. And laughingly, the two men put the goat into the dog's (we'll call him Buzzard) run and left the two together.

That night the two men came out with one pan of feed. When Buzzard dashed toward it, the goat penned him against the chain-link fence and butted him repeatedly until Buzzard escaped and ran to his house.

The two men couldn't have been more pleased. Next morning they did the same thing: fed the goat and not the dog. And once again the dog was butted into his abode.

It happened the third morning and it happened the fourth morning, and the two men were rubbing their hands in delight, slapping each other on the back and saying, "Well we've got it whipped now . . . that ol' goat's sure goin' a take Buzzard off deer."

The fifth morning they brought the goat's meal – and old Buzzard had done gone and killed that goat and ate about half of him. When they released Buzzard, he chased every deer in the county.

Water Shyness

There'll be times you want a pointing dog to retrieve game from water. But this shouldn't be Pup's first water contact. If so, forget it. Instead, Pup should have been started as a young pup Happy Timing with his kennelmates on a hot day, and then walked to water where he grudge-lessly enters and lolls and laps and maybe even rolls around like a seal. Now, this is good water love and will probably stay with Pup the rest of his life. And it's a good time to toss sticks for him to fetch to shore. We're not building a bona fide retriever here. We just want the poultry in hand any way we can get it.

If Pup was denied Happy Timing, then put him on the chain gang with no water. Go get him every hour and walk him to a creek or pond where he will lap. Then chain him again. Repeat the process over and over.

Or, take off your clothes and jump in, coaxing Pup to follow. This is especially good if you take tidbits to feed Pup when he enters and wades to you – only later make it swimming water.

And finally, get in a rowboat and start rowing from shore with the whole pack in pursuit. Pup won't be able to stick it out alone on shore—he'll jump in.

Hard Mouth

Go to the magic table coming up in the next chapter.

Eating the Bird

See the magic table.

Refusing to Retrieve or Running Away with the Bird

See the magic table.

Fighting

Two dogs in a fight can be your total calamity. When it happens, it happens fast, and you must be ready. Hopefully, you have another person with you, for both of you must each grab the hind legs of one dog and pull the two apart—only to swing each of them in great circles until they're so dizzy they can't stand. That'll stop any dogfight.

If you can't get both dogs because you're alone, then grab the aggressor by the hind legs and give him the merry-go-round.

But do it fast and forcefully, for dogs in a fight have no sense of anyone or anything. You can be bit severely. And the dog won't even know he did it.

Water can sometimes separate dogs, but that's only available in a kennel tussle. Nothing does it like the twirl.

Horse Shyness or Horse Defiance

Though there are at least two national foot-hunting bird dog test formats, still the classic bird dog field trial is horseback. Plus, this is the best way for the very young or very old, or the infirm, to enjoy a day's hunt afield. They can't walk all that well, so let the horse walk while they ride. Consequently, there are many reasons a bird dog should be reliable around horse stock.

If a dog shies from (or tries to fight) a horse, then make the horse a fact of the dog's life. Kennel him immediately beside the horse until the horse disappears. That is, until the dog finally ignores the horse, accepts him, and gives up trying to antagonize him.

Though, once again, there are some dogs that go to their graves hating and taunting horses (or shying from them). Such dogs must just be hunted on foot.

Catwalking

Some dogs catwalk right by, or on beyond, bracemates on either point or honor. When hunting alone, such barge-in dogs may crowd birds, causing a flush.

Any dog that lifts a foot in the scent cone, or moves after another dog has gone on point or taken up honor, must be physically picked up, scolded, and carried to the exact spot he vacated. Remember, dogs are very aware of place.

If the dog persists in catwalking, then he must once again be hunted with a trailing check cord. Should he break point or honor, pick him up, return him to the spot vacated, stretch out the check cord, bump him with the bowline knot, and command, "Whoa."

If the dog persists in encroachment, then take him back to the whoa post and the power bar and all the way through the basics.

Relocating

Should Pup point a bird that moves, he must relocate to keep the heat on and stop the bird from flying. Yet, Pup can't catwalk on a stationary bird. So we create a training situation where the planted bird can walk but not fly. Check-cord Pup into the area and let him establish point. Ideally, this would be mowed grass where Pup can actually see the bird move. Then seeing the bird on the walk, tell Pup, "All right," indicating he can step forward. But when Pup nears the bird, tighten the check cord and/or flip the bowline knot for Pup to whoa. He'll get the idea.

Stop to Flush

Pup must put all four feet flat and not even move an eyelid (in other words, Pup must whoa) on every bird encounter—whether the birds are sitting, walking, running, or flying. If another dog accidentally bumps birds up and they buzz Pup, he must stop. Or when working *with* the wind, Pup may inadvertently barge into birds. Again, he must stop. But should Pup be working *into* the wind and bump birds himself, then he's no longer in a stop-to-flush situation. He did not honor the birds' scent cone, worked too close, and put the birds up by his own error. That means he refused to whoa at the edge of the scent cone – which he must do – so he must be returned to all basics.

Running Livestock

Pup must be taken off livestock the same way we took him off deer. If he pursues domestic rabbits, poultry, cattle, horses, goats, or sheep, he must be put in pocket. And the way to do that is to catch him in the act and give him a mock mauling. In other words train like momma dog does. She stands above the errant pooch, her lips pursed to thin lines, her eyes aglare, her hackles raised, her ears pointed, while a growl straight from hell bubbles like hot lava in her throat. And that's what we do. We take Pup's legs from him, whack him good with the fly-swatter, and all in mock rage we yell and glare, and let the heat of our pretended rage scorch his face. One time should do it.

Dropping on Point

If Pup plops on point each time he scents a bird or drops to flush, then throw a half hitch about his flank with your check cord and hold him up.

Or you can pump him up. Just go to him and grasp his hips across his backbone with your extended thumb and little finger. Now shove. Pup will resist. Shove again. He'll rear back. Keep shoving until he's shoving back in equal pressure; keep it up until Pup's standing.

Also, you can return to the power bar and force Pup up, or work him on the whoa post. Should he sink, pump him up.

A better way is to stand Pup on a table. Should he sit, fine. Now pull him up. Then keep pulling, in short tugs. That is, you're going to pull him off the table if he doesn't take a purchase. He will. Now you've got a dog that couldn't be forced to sit with an anvil on his back. Once again, you're dealing in reverse force. Whatever you do, Pup does the opposite – all to your benefit. You pump, he raises. You tug, he tightens up and takes a stand.

Pointing Nongame

Dogs will point skunks, cats, rabbits, snakes, coons, and sometimes stinking gourds. In this instance there is nothing you can do about it, nor should you.

Some people are more narrow-minded and say feather's the game. But not to Pup. Game's game, food's food. Nothing I've mentioned hasn't at one time or another been dropped in a pot by a hungry man. A rabbit would taste as good to Pup as a quail. It's his world. You've entered it. Let him call the shots on this one.

Stealing Point

A dog that steals point is a thief without honor. He is the lowest form of sneak and – wait a minute. There's another just as low. That's a dog that will run off from his bracemate at a trial as though he's really boring a hole in the skyline only to bed up against a damp log in a cool, green place. There, he'll wait for the sound of men's *halllllloooos* and the neighs of horses before he gets up and finishes fresh and strong, showing the judges just what swell condition he's really in.

But before truth broke in I was saying, "A catwalking dog is the lowest form of sneak. . . ." He lets some old full-bored nose campaigner find the scent cone, close in, and hold the birds tight; and then this guy tippy-toes by and steals the birds. Why? Precisely because he didn't honor.

When you come on these two dogs, you'll "see" the offender is the pointing dog and the actual pointing dog is the backer. And you won't know the difference. And this is not a double find: an instance when two dogs are pointing the same covey of birds, but are out of each other's sight.

You can check on point stealing, if you become suspicious, by reading track. For Pup to steal point, he'll have to catwalk past the other dog. His track will be short-stepped, which it never would have been if he'd slammed to point from a running race.

To correct this fault, hide an aide upwind from a planted bird. It stands to reason this man cannot be seen, smelled, or heard. If he could, he would have no value. Direct your point-stealing dog and a bracemate into the area while you lag to rear, out of sight. The hope is the bracemate makes the point. Should Pup take a step to break honor, the concealed aide will break cover, coming in a scream, whomping Pup good and then putting him precisely in the place where he moved from.

Always remember, dogs have a powerful sense of place. Then when you come near, you complete the act by bawling out Pup yourself.

Or let the aide stay out of sight and unheard while you ride or walk on in. Saying nothing, go directly to Pup; pick him up and place him in the precise spot the aide (who now appears) tells you. Forever after Pup will wonder who's in the brush. He can never trust an empty quail field again. There will always be the possibility of someone there. This will help mend his errant ways. Repeat the drill until it does.

Chasing Cars

At no time should Pup run loose so he can chase a car. This is a junkyard-dog pursuit. Not our Pup. But let's say he does chase cars. Well, there are several ways to handle this. Have the driver come past, let Pup give chase, then have an assistant in the car dump a bucket of water on Pup. That'll make him think.

If Pup persists and you want to go the distance, then tie rags onto your wheels. Let them flap. Now Pup will grab these when they go past and get the flop of his life. But it may kill him, remember that. Like I said, "If you really want to go the distance." For sure it'll take Pup off chasing cars.

And finally, have the car stop and the aide jump out brandishing a white flyswatter – Pup'll think the world's filled with these things – and he'll come high-tailing home with the cursing guy in pursuit. You're always Pup's savior. You get him quickly to safe haven and drive off the intruder, who's never seen again, and Pup's left wondering.

Cribbing

If Pup's eating his doghouse to splinters, or mutilating the chain link in his kennel run, or flat shredding water buckets and just leaving that little steel ring that runs around the crimped top, then you've got a bored dog. There's only one solution. Work him.

Digging

Like the cribber, the digger is also bored. Activity is the only solution. But there are two preventions for a kennel-kept dog. Pour a concrete run (Pup can't dig in concrete), or bury his fence so deep in dirt he can't reach bottom. The deep fence may not stop the digging, but it will prevent Pup from leaving and eventually frustrate him from even trying to dig out.

Barking

The kennel-kept dog presents the best situation to hush a barking dog. Install a store-bought or homemade sound detector that triggers an overhead shower. You can install it yourself. Run water pipe over the top of the kennel runs, install shower heads over each run, attach the valve to a solenoid triggered by a sound detector, and you're in business.

If Pup is a house dog (and I hope he is), then the white flyswatter kept by the door is your answer. Plus, there are several things that will trigger Pup, and I know what they are: the meter reader, the UPS truck, and the garbage truck. Know when these culprits are coming by and be ready. The flyswatter – just showing it – will do the trick.

Bump And Run

There's a fault generally seen in young dogs (if it's going to occur), and that's bumping shoulders with other dogs as they are released for a breakaway. Rather than hunt, they bounce until they decide to stop and flat fight it out. There's one cure. That's to run these dogs apart from each other. Especially run them (one at a time) with an older dog that won't put up with this nonsense. Two dyed-in-the-wool bump and runs will keep at it until they get too old for such play. By then, you're sick of the lot of them.

So just never run them together.

6

The Magic Table

MOST ANY RETRIEVER will retrieve: that's not really the point. Will he retrieve in the most adverse conditions? Will he break ice, swim into a northern with duck in mouth and waves splashing over his head? Or work a torrid stand of cattails for early-fall teal when he'd rather be out in the open, taking the breezes or lying beside a block of ice? Or pick up something that offends him and bring it to you? Or come from water and hold the duck while he shakes? Or have to stool on a retrieve but never drop the bird while he attends to his toilet?

Will he be able to endure the commotion of going hunting? That is, the barking guns, the falling birds, and the shouting men. Can he withstand being a cartage service? Doing the drawn-out, boring job of canine shuttle of dead ducks. Poor Pup. He pulls into each corner like a weary bus driver, picks up his fares, and delivers them to where they're going, while he turns off the madcap parade of fun-makers.

Or finally, will he make a sure'nuf retrieve after a long day's hunt with his belly worn raw by row-crop stubble when you cast him for one last bird shot down?

Well, a natural retriever can quit you. But a dog that's graduated from the magic table will never let you down. And if by some quirk he does, there's something you can do about it to guarantee performance.

So that's what we'll handle in this chapter: guaranteed retriever performance. I don't care if you send Pup for a bull snake, your blown-off hat, or a bona fide waterfowl cripple – Pup'll fetch it up. Showing how it's done starts now.

But just a minute. I didn't give this device and this technique that goes with it the name "magic" to be quaint. I named it so because "magic" is exactly what it is. You think it'll teach retrieving – and it will. But it will do so much more.

That's the way with all good training devices. They give back more than you put in, or even think of putting in. Like the chain gang. That device helps us cure so many faults. And so does the magic table.

You've heard the expression, "He needs an attitude talk"? Well, that's what the magic table delivers. You put a renegade dog up there and he'll become such a good citizen he could run for mayor. And the dowdy dog, the doubting dog – put him up there, and in two weeks he'll have his chest puffed out and be asking around, "Anyone want to make my day?" And finally the fighter. Put him up there and he'll put away his dukes for good.

Recently it has come to pass that some trainers are putting more than one dog on the table at the same time; and they're getting the same results we saw when working the golden triangle of dogs. All that intercommunication is at work to bold up the wallflower, tame down the maverick, and place at peace the pugnacious.

Building the Magic Table

First, you build the table, and you build it stout. Nothing flimsy. This table's going to take some stress, and it has to be built to last. There's

High-class equipment rigs up this guy's magic table. The turnbuckle is of radically new design, and the trolley looks built for the job. Yet, the whole thing is held together with bailing wire. Just go the way it suits you.

nothing complicated about the construction, and you can substitute materials as you please. Since I first introduced the magic table in 1977, I've seen these tables made of every conceivable grouping of materials. I've seen tables that ranged from the slipshod to the exotic. Some are slum tables; others are Trump Towers.

The table measures as follows: you want it as high as your belt (which means each table is built expressly for the trainer who'll use it) and at least three feet wide. Make the table as long as possible. I've seen store-bought, collapsible picnic tables used that are six feet in length. I've seen pros create a table by covering individual dog houses along a row in the kennel. Let's say they had thirty runs measuring three feet across. That gave them a magic table ninety feet long.

Centered at each end of this table is an upright stake—a two-by-four, steel post, T-post, or what have you. These posts must be super-rigid. They bear all the stress. Between these posts you run a length of steel cable, secured to each end with turnbuckles so the whole thing can be wound up taut. When using wood posts, you also must run a beam of wood between the tops of the two legs to keep them from collapsing inward.

Before you secure each end of the cable, slip on a couple of rolling trolleys. Ideally, you'd use ball-bearing trolleys, but I've also seen some things as cheap as a looped piece of rope run on there: just keep the cable soaped good for ease of movement. From these trolleys is dropped a piece of rope; better yet a series of snap swivels (each connected to the other) so each dog can be custom-fitted (in height) when placed on the table and under the cable.

Test your table to make sure it's going to hold, and run your trolleys back and forth to make sure they're free-wheeling.

Now, go get your dog and make sure he is wearing a flat nylon or leather collar with a strong, welded D-ring to which you attach a snap swivel. If you think the dog is going to fight, run a rope from a second trolley around his flank. Now you've got him "hooked up" in two places: throat and flank.

Okay, on to the philosophy of the magic table and teaching retrieve.

To insert something into a dog's mouth, he must open his mouth. It's that simple. And for centuries man has tried every conceivable way to get the dog's mouth open. Trainers have pinched ears with their thumbnails; they have squeezed paws; and they actually have forced open the mouth by digging a thumb between the jaws. And in every case they were wrong.

Wrong for two main reasons. First, they had their hands on the dog. We train with our head (as much as possible), not our hand.

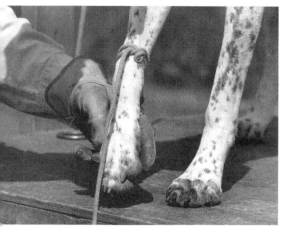

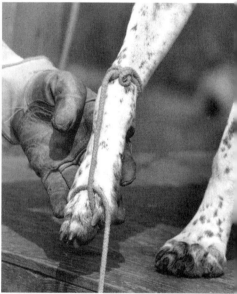

A nerve cord is attached with a clove hitch to the leg above the carpal joint.

It hangs straight down between the dog's two center toes. There the knot is wrapped one time about itself, and the nerve hitch is complete.

Second, besides touching the dog, they were inflicting lasting pain. They were even maiming the dog. I've seen more than one old warrior with permanent scarring on his ears. What we need is something that delivers excruciating pain to get the dog to say *OUCH*—which he can only say if he *opens his mouth*—but then *immediately* the pain is removed and there is no lasting imprint, no residual scarring.

Our device to accomplish all this is called a nerve hitch. We build a nerve hitch out of a six-foot length of one-eighth-inch nylon cord. It was observed centuries ago that if you count over three toes (from inside to out), you can press in the cavity where that toe touches the paw and trigger a nerve. Admittedly, some dogs are more sensitive than others. So we took our nerve-hitch cord and tied it in a clove hitch just above the knee, let it drop straight down over the two inside toes, wrapped it about these two toes, tied it in a simple half-hitch, pulled on it, and the dog said *OUCH*. *Eureka!* Now we've got the dog opening his mouth so we can insert a dowel that will substitute for our bird in preliminary training.

Tie that nerve-hitch cord to the right leg, if you're a right-handed gunner, and vice versa. We'll discuss the reason later.

Are you ready?

Introducing the Dowel

Okay, put Pup on the magic table, snap him to a trolley, and let him settle. Let him roam about if that's what he wants. Some dogs will jump off and hang there. Don't rush to them. They can climb back on themselves – and they will. The reason we ignore his plight is we want Pup to know he's in this thing *alone* for the duration. And the only way he can come off that table is through compliance – through fetching.

Now, don a pair of leather work gloves. Go to Pup with a dowel in your hand. Just a minute, you say, what's a dowel? Well, it's a nine-inch section cut from the handle of whatever hickory or oak garden tool

A dowel is inserted in the dog's mouth while handler says coolly, "Hold it, hold it." But there's one thing wrong with this photo. Know what it is? The dog's collar is too low on his neck. It should be up where the man's right hand grasps the collar with his two center fingers while his thumb automatically goes up into the space between the bones of the dog's lower jaw.

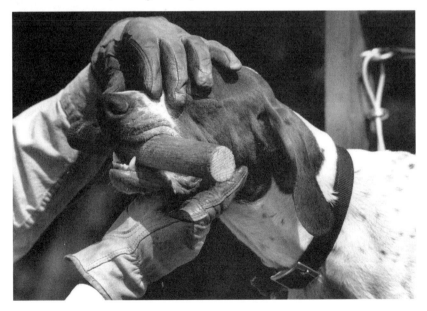

failed last. We want hard wood so Pup can't bite down and indent it. Not only are we teaching guaranteed retrieving, but we're also getting rid of hard mouth.

Now take your left hand (if you're a right-handed gunner) and span it across Pup's muzzle. Gently squeeze between the jaws until Pup opens his mouth; immediately insert the dowel, which is always held horizontal and directly before Pup's nose. Quickly reach up with your right hand and insert your flat fingers under Pup's collar with your upright thumb wedging into the V of his lower jaw. Now you've got the bottom jaw immobilized (the only jaw that can move), and you begin grooming Pup's mouth with your left hand. You see, there's a specific place we want this dowel to sit.

Take a pencil and put it in your mouth. Shove it back. Uncomfortable? You bet it is. Now let the pencil come forward where it rests just behind your canine teeth. Okay? Sure it is. You could hold that pencil there all day. And that's where we want the dowel in Pup's mouth. We want Pup comfortable, relaxed. Also, pull out the lips. We don't want them pinched. Then love Pup with your left hand, stroking him, telling him what a fine boy he is. Then saying, "Leave it," push the dowel forward into Pup's mouth, twist it at the same time, and take it from him.

Most people make a mistake when taking a bird to hand. They pull instead of push. Pulling makes Pup hard mouth, sticky mouth. To pull is to leave part of the carcass in Pup's mouth and the rest in your hand. So, you always push the dowel (this gags Pup) and twist it (this releases his tooth hold on the wood) and he spits out the dowel. I've had you say, "Leave it." You can also say, "Give," or whatever command fits your fancy.

Do this over and over; press the jaws apart, insert the dowel, groom, hold the jaw steady with the angle of your thumb, tell Pup how great he is, then say, "Give," and push while you twist.

Incidentally, while you're cutting one dowel from that discarded garden tool, cut three more. You'll now have one presented before Pup's nose and three more in your right hand (if you're a right-handed gunner) rear pocket. Pup can never be successful in spitting the dowel out. Should he actually do this, immediately another is presented from your pocket, and Pup begins to see the futility of fighting you.

Also, should Pup really be giving you a time on that table by rearing back and leaping sideways and even trying to bite you – then run the flank strap about his waist to further secure him and keep him under control.

This dog's really fetching. Note how far his neck extends from the table to take the dowel upon the command fetch. *Note the box beneath Pup's right front foot. That's a love table, where dogs are fondled before and after a session with the nerve hitch. It may be the most important training asset you ever build.*

The Nerve Hitch

We've kept up our dowel presentation until we're sick of it, and Pup's accepting it. Fine. Now we go to the real thing. Present the dowel with your right hand (if you're a right-handed gunner) before Pup's nose and reach down and pick up the trailing nerve-hitch cord. Now say, "Fetch," and pull the cord, which transmits the pain, which causes Pup to rear back and squeal in protest. Immediately you insert the dowel, while at the *very same time* you drop the nerve-hitch cord. Then you do several things at once. You reach up with your left hand and loosen the cord (if it's tightened about Pup's toes and won't release) while you hold the dowel in Pup's mouth with your right hand. Then immediately up comes your left hand to seat the dowel and groom Pup's mouth while the right hand settles in the plain, flat collar and the angle of the thumb naturally centers into the V of Pup's bottom jaw.

Again you tell Pup what a great guy he is, and you groom him and love him and coo to him all kinds of wonderful compliments.

Then saying, "Give," you immediately push the dowel into Pup's mouth, twist, and remove it.

If a dog tries to manhandle a trainer, he can be tied up about the waist and short-tied at the neck. Now the handler has greater control.

Now you're ready to do it all over again. But I must admit it's not always this simple. Oh, you'll have a ton of dogs comply – some won't even resist – but you'll have others that go crazy.

And sometimes having the flank tied with the rope won't help you, and you'll have to do this: have a table shoved up into the corner of a barn or a garage. Put two eye bolts in the wall. Tie Pup's leather collar to one bolt, tie a tight flank strap to the other. Now Pup is literally tied to the wall. Then go through your presentation of the dowel, the pull of the nerve-hitch cord, the insertion of the dowel, the moment Pup says OUCH, the release of the cord, and the grooming of the mouth.

If Pup proves to be a committed fighter, then gather other dogs around. Their presence can soothe him. Eventually Pup'll let his milk down, and you can return him to the regular magic table. There you'll continue with the standard nerve-hitch drill.

The Dummy

It's all worthwhile to be standing there presenting the dowel to Pup, and have him getting to the place where he physically reaches for it at the first indication you're going to pull the nerve-hitch cord. But Pup

Note this box of bucks. Even though these are made of hard oak, the dogs have imprinted them with their teeth.

doesn't fetch from a stationary position. He casts, goes forth, finds the dead bird, scoops it up, and returns it to you for delivery to hand. So that's what we'll start now.

Those of you who don't want to change your gear that much (and thus disturb Pup) can take one of your dowels and convert it to a buck. A buck is a dowel with pegs attached to each end so they form ninety-degree angles. So rigged, no matter how you throw the buck, it'll land upright with the dowel elevated from the ground, and Pup can more easily get the thing in his mouth.

You make a buck by drilling two holes in each end of the dowel with a drill press. Drill the holes opposite to each other. Through these holes insert four- to five-inch-pegs. The result is a device that looks like a miniature tank trap or a child's jack (that goes with the bouncing ball, remember?).

Now take this buck to the far end of your table, set Pup up, and take the nerve-hitch cord, Pup's leather collar, or the swivel snaps in your left hand. Lead Pup down the table, telling him to fetch or saying, "Dead bird." When Pup gets to the buck, chances are good he'll automatically reach for the thing. If not, pull the nerve-hitch cord, and Pup will frantically search for anything to take to mouth to stop the pain. *Eureka!* He grabbed the buck.

Now walk Pup back to his "sit" position – all the while Pup's carrying the buck – as you tell him, "Hold it, hold it, hold it . . ." When you get him to his original spot, tell him "Sit," and then, pushing and twisting the buck in Pup's mouth, command him to "Give," or "Leave it." Cheers, for Pup's just made his first retrieve.

Keep running him on this drill, over and over. Day after day. Week after week. When you think Pup's got it – go another week, two weeks, or a month. Why the extra time? We're looking for two things. First, we want Pup to jut his jaw out and grab for the upheld dowel just by our saying the command "Fetch." Second, before we're completely finished,

See how Pup favors his nerve-hitch leg as he goes for a distant dummy on the table. Mike Gould applies little pressure, yet Pup wants it off and off fast. Makes for a speedy performer.

Pup will be doing all this with a wagging tail. That's the tip-off and the finish. The wagging tail. Same applies to most drills.

But let's say you're not that concerned whether Pup stays with the oak or hickory dowel or fetching something else. Okay, switch to a small boat bumper (or dummy). You know, those things you hang on the side of your boat so it won't rub against the dock. Cast Pup (or walk him down) for the dummy. Yes, later you'll be casting Pup by telling him "All right" or reaching out and tapping him on the back of his head. By then he'll be running to the end of the table, and you'll not need to walk him there. By then you order him to come when he has the dummy in his mouth, and he'll finish his retrieve. The sequence will be your saying "All right" as you tap Pup to cast; Pup will do so, and as he turns you say, "Come"; and as he does, you continually caution him to "Hold it." Then when he's finally in front of you, order him to "Give" or "Leave it," and you've finished the sequence.

Introduction to the Bird

Now comes the bird, be it frozen quail or pigeon. Frozen? Yes. We're still fighting hard mouth, and Pup'll no more bite down on a frozen bird than you will (generally) on an ice cube.

Note: we want a bloodless, frozen bird to combat both hard mouth and sticky mouth. To get a bloodless bird, put it in a paper sack, seal it, and wait for the bird to go to sleep. Then, and this is important, groom the bird's feet so the toenails are tucked up and inward. They are very sharp; and if Pup hit them just right it might make him bird shy. Get them out of mouth's range.

Okay, lay the bird on the end of the table and cast Pup for it. You can first introduce Pup to it if you want, the way we did the dowel. Just

Dummy, buck, what have you, is now taken to earth, and Pup is asked to fetch immediately beside the magic table. Let's use all the association we can get.

Here Mike helps Pup make a fetch by kicking him along with the nerve-hitch cord.

open his mouth, insert the bird, groom the lips, and stand there, telling Pup, "Hold it." Either way, Pup will be walked down the table to the waiting bird, told to fetch it up, will be pinched with the nerve hitch if he hesitates to comply, then told, "Hold it," as you walk Pup back to his original position.

The Good Earth

Now we take Pup from the table for his moment of truth. But I advise you, work him immediately before the table so the table is always in Pup's mind—don't go somewhere afield. Lay a dummy, a buck, or a frozen bird in the distance, and go through the regular sequence with Pup. Walk him down and all that. Later, when this has been successfully accomplished, you'll stand in one place, cast Pup toward the bird, and wait for his return. He just soloed. Please remember, we're teaching bird dogs, not retrievers, to retrieve. That's an entirely different process on the cast, and we'll go there shortly.

Pup Fetching Afield

Now we go to the actual bird down and a dog cast. You hunt Pup into the bird's scent cone, skirt him, kick up the bird, shoot, kill the bird, watch it fall, then release Pup by standing beside him and giving him the tap on his head.

But what if Pup won't go? That's hardly likely, but we'll cover that rare event anyway. You see, Pup's still wearing his nerve-hitch cord. It's just not laced around his toes. It merely hangs from the clove hitch knot tied above Pup's carpal joint. All you have to do is reach over, pick up the end of that cord, and all the lights will come on in Pup's head. Hold the cord in your right hand (if you're a right-handed gunner) and tap Pup's head with your left hand. Pup'll go.

But being the devil's advocate, let's say he still refuses to cast for a fetch. In this case, hold the cord in your right hand—it now goes across your body—and catch it with the heel of your left boot. When you raise your left arm and tap Pup's head to fetch, you also kick out your left boot, catapulting Pup from his sitting position. For the tug upon the carpal joint now has the same force as hand-pulling the nerve hitch.

Or if it's not all that serious, and Pup's just dawdling, then merely tap his right foot with your left boot, saying, "Fetch," and I'll bet you a Purdy shotgun against a short .22 rifle he explodes out of there like a missile.

So That's About It

We're just about finished teaching Pup how to fetch, but there are a couple of things you ought to know. Should Pup freeze – either on the table or in the field – and not want to give up the bird (and you both push and twist and he still holds tight), there are two things you can do. First, reach over and take your index finger and hook it into the skin coming from the leg at the flank. Literally lift Pup off the ground with that flap of skin, and he'll be more than glad to give you the bird. Second, get down and blow a blast of air into Pup's nose – especially effective if you're smoking a cigar. By taking Pup's air away, he'll gulp, and you grab the bird. Never, never get into a wrestling match. You'll just have to go back to the magic table to work on hard mouth.

As the months advance you can eventually take the nerve-hitch cord off Pup's carpal joint when running afield. But wad it up and keep it stored in your coat pocket. Should Pup fail you, just produce the cord and dangle it in front of him. He'll know. You bet your life he'll know, and he'll correct his ways.

But be respectful of this. Pup can be sent to get a strong cripple where he'll have to both run and leap to catch it. Should he break a bird bone, be considerate. Or if you shoot a bird too close and render it hamburger – and Pup comes upon this riddled morsel and gets sticky mouth – remember, it was your fault (you shot too quick), and not Pup's.

So always shoot to kill, and always shoot at proper range. You and Pup are a team, and it's your responsibility to think ahead to keep him out of predicaments. It is also your responsibility to help Pup mark the point of a bird's fall. Help him. Go to that spot and keep Pup from straying. Have him pinpointed, and keep him there for a successful fetch.

7

Wrapping Up

SO, WE'VE CORRECTED most faults that plague the average bird dog and confront the average trainer. And we did it hands off, never touching the dog except when it was mighty necessary, tapping him with a simple, lightweight, white plastic flyswatter. There was no shouting, stomping, kicking, beating, shooting, shocking, or in any way brutalizing Pup to get him off his errant ways and on to a new (and much better) life.

For I want you to remember this. *When a dog makes you mad, he's defeated you.* And that's the last thing that can happen. Think out the scenario. If Pup can't be cured, he's worthless; and if he's worthless, he'll more than likely be put down by you or some branch of the humane society. So you actually have the opportunity to let Pup live and to make that life a good one. One filled with happiness and achievement and good feelings because he's no longer a problem dog. Now he's a bona fide bird dog because you were his problem-solver.

But how many trainers have gone on not to solve Pup's problem but, instead, to become his additional and eventual back-breaking problem?

It all matters whether you have the innate genius, common courtesy to life, and patience to see a dog through his crisis. For crisis is what it is. The dog did not want to arrive at this state—someone drove him there. For we'll all remember John Nash's observation, "There are no such things as bad pups . . . just bad dogs." And the only thing that happened to make the difference is man. And the only thing that can happen to unmake that difference is thoughtful man.

Now you are one. Let's get on to retrievers.

PART THREE

THE
RETRIEVERS

8

The Retrievers

WE NOW MOVE on to the retrievers. Here we deal with an entirely different critter than the bird dogs. You see, the bird dogs descended from pack dogs perfecting carnal instincts. They have a latent tendency to chase and kill in order to eat. But the retrievers are far more removed from the pack motivation. They are companion dogs, like the shepherds, and they work best one on one. In contrast, the pointers work excellently in a pack, like their cousins, the hounds.

We see what I'm talking about when we examine the classic relationship of the elk and the wolf. The wolves jump, harass, and drive the elk in far-dispersed packs using uncanny communication between the members of the pack, which can stretch out over a half mile – communication necessary to determine direction, pace, state of the chased herd's psyche, and where the weakest animal is.

Sure, all domesticated dogs descended from the wolf. But they came to us through different routings with different relationships with man. The caveman could well use the pack dog to drive and hedge in and bay or even kill game. But the men of the sea who developed the retrievers sought a companion dog for close living on a boat, as well as the ability to follow instructions given over a relatively near distance. Also, that work did not deal with killing, but with retrieving inanimate objects – such as ropes.

A hunting Lab lays pheasant harvest in snow.

The result? The bird dog has the latent tendencies to be a bolter (a chaser) and a killer (he'll chomp a bird good if he hasn't been on the magic table). But the retriever is a mellow fellow, more inclined to share the man's meal than to go kill one for his own.

"You've got to know the nature of the beast" is a common saying that nowhere has more applicability than it does here. The bird dog trainer's primary hardship is to control over long distance. The retriever trainer must concentrate with control of a companion animal near to side or not too far away. The bird dog trainer, if you will, must work to take the killer out of the dog, whereas the retriever trainer must work to instill the spirit that would ordinarily go with killing.

One trainer has to hold down his charge, the other has to pump his up.

Traditionally, the retriever taken to the gun has been a nonslip performer. That is, the collar was not slipped off the dog so he could make his retrieve until after the game was killed. But a movement that began in 1983 has changed all this. We now have the hunting re-triever—the dog whose duties have now been expanded to include hunting out, flushing up, waiting for the kill, then either retrieving the deadfall or searching out the runaway cripple. So, now more than ever, it is imperative that man put back some of the killing instinct in the retriever; rather than being a passive dog that just fetches up what's shot, he now goes out and drives the bird to shot, then chases it down if it tries to get away.

In the pages that follow we'll correct faults of both retriever types: the classic field-trial retriever and the new hunter. It's the classic field-trial retriever that poses the most problems because man has asked him to perform tasks that require the dog to ignore his own instincts. To get a living thing to go against its own nature usually calls for brutality in training—something I will not do.

We'll still teach these retrievers to perform meaningless tests that have nothing to do with hunting, and we'll do it with hands off—no whipping, shouting, shooting, or shocking.

I'll give you an example. The classic field-trial circuit demands a retriever run a water blind (go get a bird he hasn't seen fall) by running him through hazards. The rule will be that the dog cannot touch land; if he does, he's out of the trial. So the bird is planted in a pond that has the configuration of a figure eight. The bird is planted in the top circle. The dog is cast from the bottom circle. He must go through the hour-glass pinch of land—the figure eight is not closed in the middle—and get the bird without touching land.

But what would the practical hunting dog do, since land is his natural route to fetch? He would run down the side of the two circles; and when he was as close to the bird as he could get, dive in. Both dogs would get the bird, but the hunting dog would do it faster and more sensibly. The classic field-trial performer forgoes good hunting sense to show he is subject to the will of man, who stands back there blow-ing his whistle and waving his arms. The classic field-trial retriever has little to do with hunting. He's more a circus performer showing exces-sive suppression of instinct and self-will. He's more of a subjugation of God's intention. He's been replaced with a man-made dog.

And man-made dogs come up with all sorts of faults. Faults, never-theless, that I must show you how to cure. For you may want to run in these trials or at least have a hunting dog that can approximate some of the antics displayed by the classic field-trial retriever.

So let's get to it. But first let me instruct you: I'll often have you turn back to techniques explained for pointing dogs, for they will be applicable. And yes, it is very valuable to know how to train all bird dogs even though you'll probably stay with only one class throughout your life. There is much transference the average pro—let alone the amateur—ignores. It is a fact of life that most men know how to train only one type of dog. It would be like knowing how to deal with only one race of people. That'd be rough—and mighty impractical— wouldn't it? So you who are interested in training only retrievers and have turned to this section first—go to the front of the book. If not, I'll lose you. You must read everything printed between these covers to train the dog of your choice.

Heel, Sit, Stay, Come

Once again we return to Mike Gould's power bar. Remember, bird dog people do not want their dogs to sit, nor to stay (which is their whoa). But this is an essential part of the retriever's makeup and his principal duties. So here we'll concentrate.

Each power bar is custom-fitted; rig one for your own frame with a twenty-foot check cord and attach the snap swivel to the welded D-ring of Pup's flat collar. Place Pup to your left (if you're a right-handed gunner), and telling him, "Heel," step off. Pup'll follow. If not, tap the power bar or the snap swivel forward. If Pup rears back, tap him up so his ear is even with your outside pants seam. If Pup jumps to side, tap him in. If he crowds your left knee, push him out. If he lunges ahead, tap him back.

When he's walking well beside you, stop, still saying, "Heel," and when he does stop, say, "Sit." Now this will be new material for us. To get a Lab to sit—wait a minute. I'll be using the terms retriever and Lab interchangeably. In my mind, they're synonymous. Dogs trained in this section include Labrador retrievers, Chesapeake Bay retrievers, golden retrievers, flat-coated retrievers, curly-coated retrievers, Irish water spaniels, American water spaniels, and any dog that will fetch.

As I was saying: to get a Lab to sit, pivot your upper body so the left hand goes back toward Pup's tail. Now lower the right hand end of the power bar, dropping down, say, level with Pup's nose. The left end of the power bar is kept high. Now push back. The power of the bar will force Pup's head up and his rear end down. He will sit. He has no alternative. It works like magic. Holding Pup there, gradually relax your pressure and continue to tell him, over and over, "Sit."

Then shake it all off, order him to heel, and step off. So now we have Pup going in right-hand circles and sitting.

Let's reverse it. Remember, to get a Lab handled by a right-handed gunner to go left, you must position the power bar parallel to earth and lay it across your lap. Extend the left-hand end of the power bar out to push Pup away from your left leg – which he naturally will be crowding as you make your left-hand turn. Now say, "Heel," and go in your left-hand circle, only to stop, once again saying, "Heel," and then, "Sit." Once again, drop the right-hand end of the power bar so your hand is even with Pup's nose – your left hand stays in natural position – and push the power bar back toward Pup's tail. He will sit.

Now tell him, "Heel," and step off, going either left or right. Then tell him to sit. Keep mixing it up and doing it over and over until Pup is fail-safe.

Now while we're doing yard work with retrievers, we must also release them for Happy Timing. Take one dog, or your whole pack, to field and let 'em rip. Let 'em bang each other and thump across rickety foot bridges and burst through bramble and chase dickeybirds and leap to water and fetch up box turtles and chase rabbits and roll in cow manure. In other words, let them have kindergarten recess. You stay out of their space. Let the day and the play be theirs. You're just along to proctor – from a distance. Then call them all in, load them up, and take them home. Back to more heel and sit, *ad infinitum*.

Remember, all work and no play makes Pup a very dull dog. And remember even more so, *you can take the spirit out of a retriever, but you can't put it back in*. All retriever training must be an even mixture of restraint, then freedom; conformance, then liberation.

Once Pup's sitting, we can teach stay. Pup's been pushed back by the power bar, and he's seated; now you step forward and face Pup – your face serious, your voice stern – as you say, "Stay." Hold up a hand like a traffic cop (this will be your hand signal) and say over and over, "Stay."

Should Pup start to move forward, make his disobedience your command. Say, "Come," and then, "Heel." And run through the process again, finally getting Pup to sit.

Now once again step before Pup (hand up, voice stern), as you command, "Stay." Should he try to move – you'll know when he's thinking about it: the muscles in his shoulder will have to roll before he can lift a foot – then you step forward and press down on the power bar. How can you do that, you say?

Well, when you step forward from now on, you drop the power bar so the right-hand end goes to earth and forms a wedge between the dirt and the D-ring on Pup's flat collar. If Pup tried to step forward, the angle of the bar would wedge him to a stop. Only now when you say, "Stay," you take your left foot and press it down on the angled power bar, transmitting power to the D-ring. Every time you say, "Stay," you press the bar with your foot.

Okay, you've got a twenty-foot rope. So now you start to back off, the bar wedging Pup between collar and earth. You keep your hand up, your voice stern, all the while saying, "Stay." When you've reached the end of your rope you yell, "Come," and flip the check cord to lift the bar from its bite in the ground and hand over hand reel Pup into you.

Here's what you now have taught: heel, sit, stay, come. Keep doing it all over and over. It is a magnificent way of training. And I've never seen a training device, other than the chain gang or the magic table, accomplish so many things as the power bar.

When you think Pup has it all down pat, stay with it another month. And keep interspersing yard training with Happy Timing. Pup's under stress, tightly controlled, totally dominated. Let him throw the whole mess off by running wild and free in the fields.

So what have you taught? I once heard an old pro say, "If you can get a dog to stop and come when called, then you can take him hunting and kill birds over him." We've done this. But there's much more we must do. Yet be proud of yourself for the progress you and Pup have made. You're probably as far along right now as most men who take a retriever hunting. For I can truly say, there isn't one hunter out of 10,000 who takes a trained dog to field. They take what they got, and what they got they never trained.

9

Problems with Marks

YOU'LL RECALL MY saying, "All dog training is like fitting links in a chain. Link A is attached to link B, link B is attached to link C, and so on." Consequently, if we develop a problem in marking, for example, or lining (going for a bird the dog has not seen fall), or even fetching, we're usually well advised to start all over from the beginning. Anyway, that's always been my practice and my philosophy. Maybe it came from boxing and wrestling so much in the Marine Corps and in college. Like in wrestling: First you go for a half nelson; then, with the leverage of that hold, you can turn the guy from his stomach to his back for a pin. Without the half nelson, it would be like turning a whale.

But the usual basic in introducing marks is for the handler to throw out a dummy (or boat bumper or bird). But let's analyze that practice. What bird have you ever seen fly from a man's hand on a day's hunt afield. None, unless you hunt with Mandrake the Magician. So I never like hand-thrown dummies: especially in the beginning.

Instead, I want the first dummy thrown to be introduced on a level, mowed-grass field. Straight away and not too far. Using big, fat, stark white dummies. Now we've given Pup every benefit of the doubt. Plus, I want that dummy thrown by a bird boy: someone afield who

The text says to start Pup on marks with white dummies. That's right. But this is an advanced dog, so the handler is using a hobbled pigeon (above the truck). Pup works a mowed-grass field where everything is very visible.

will *hurrah* to get Pup's attention (or blow a duck call if you're training a hunting retriever). The bird boy then will loft the bird while he fires (or does not fire) a training pistol and you send Pup to fetch.

Breaking

The first hazard in all this is for Pup to break. He won't wait for the bird to be thrown, or he won't wait for it to land, or he won't wait after it's landed for you to line him up and cast him for the fetch.

And why not? Well, we didn't stay long enough with our heel, sit, stay, drill. See why I say all dog training is placing links in a chain? Now we've got to go back to yard training. It's just that simple. And it's just that wasteful of time and effort. You should have stayed with your yard drill until you were sure Pup had it. But I understand. We all want to get done in five minutes what it should take a year to do. Like

Handler tells Pup to mark with extended left hand. Note that his right hand holds the check cord, which was run through the D-ring of Pup's collar.

Pup waits out thrown mark of bird boy, so the handler lets him go fetch by casting him and releasing the slip cord so it slides through the D-ring.

this book. I'm sitting here typing away, watching the months go by. Wouldn't it be great to just let 'er rip and let the words fall where they may and get the thing done and published?

But no, that wouldn't be right. I would have left out a link. I would have forgotten. Or I wouldn't have explained something fully or descriptively. So I labor word after word, peck after peck. For that's the only way the book can be written, just as that's the only way the dog can be trained. So if I use up the year it takes to write the book, then you use up the year it takes to train Pup. You'd be miffed if I shirked my job, just as Pup is miffed if you shirk yours.

Okay, it's back to the power bar drill: heel, sit, stay, come. But I can help you a little. I call it my two-idiot drill.

Sure, you sometimes hunt alone, but usually there's someone with you. Plus, at a field trial or a hunt test (a hunt test is what the hunting retriever clubs call their field trials) there'll be at least one judge standing behind you and Pup at the casting line. So let's use this fellow hunter or this judge. Let's use him to keep Pup from breaking.

Get yourself two high school football players (guys fast and strong) and position them behind Pup. Call for the bird. Should Pup break, then have the two idiots break, too. They'll come forward like wild men—waving their arms, shouting, and coming down heavy-footed—and they'll grab Pup: to roll him over and mock-maul him and shout down in his face and just make him think they're going to kill him. As always, you are Pup's benefactor, his protector, his savior. Mildly, softly, you come forward and remove Pup's attackers and dispatch them to stand behind the casting line.

Now you and Pup line up again for the bird to be thrown. But when the bird boy *hurrahs* and displays the bird, and then throws it to air either to fire the blank pistol or not—Pup will sit there, looking back, fear in his eyes, for he'll not know what the two idiots are going to do. When you softly send Pup for the bird, he hesitates a moment, making sure it's all right to finally cast.

But always after this mock-mauling Pup will wonder if the guys along for the hunt or those standing around at the trial are going to jump him for breaking—and he'll mend his ways.

Something else you can do is fit Pup with a slip lead. Take a six-, eight-, or ten-foot length of ⅜-inch nylon cord; tie one end to your belt and run the loose end through Pup's welded D-ring and back across your body to your right hand (if you're a right-handed gunner). Should Pup stay when the bird is thrown, cast him with your left hand, giving the oral signal, "Back," and sweeping your left hand up beside his face like you were throwing a bowling ball. But just a minute, what's this "Back"? Well, that's a term inherited from Great Britain where hunters used to stop their retrievers in the field, then raise their arms and command, "Back." In other words, "Get on back." The word has now become part of our retriever lexicon. When we want to cast the dog, we tell him to *back*. That's just the way it is.

Okay. Pup stayed, and you let him run out with the check cord sliding through his D-ring because you released the end of the cord held in your right hand. But what if Pup broke? Then you would have held the cord in your right hand, and Pup would have gone head over teacup. And that's another way to stop a dog from breaking.

The dog on the right must honor, so in the beginning the handler blocks his view of the running dog. The bird boy at field throws a bird and hurrahs, *and the running dog casts. The honoring dog sits downcast, for he cannot have the fun.*

Still another way is to have the bird boy beat Pup to the bird — while you yell Pup down and take a bird secreted in your training jacket and display it before him. He'll come running back. Do this enough and Pup'll always wonder if there isn't an easier bird to get right out of your hand. Plus, you'll confuse him. He'll be wondering where birds are going to come from next, which causes him to hesitate. Bird dog trainers use this to keep a dog steady on point after the birds have flushed. It looks good to the judges. The gun has fired, the birds have all flown away, and Pup stands there only to hear the gun fire once again and a bird appear from nowhere. It also keeps a bird dog from breaking — he lingers now, waiting to be sent for the fetch, for there may be another bird coming up.

And finally, we keep a retriever from breaking by snapping him to a large O-bolt screwed into the U-shaped cutout in the front of a dog box. A dog box is placed beside the duck blind (or pit) while the gunner hunts, then when he wants to pick up the birds, he reaches over, unsnaps the snap swivel, and tells Pup, "Back." The U-shaped cutout accommodates Pup's neck – lets him stick his head out and see what's going on. The box can be open or closed; it can also be toted along as a car kennel, or even into a motel room where Pup can be snapped to sleep out the night.

Honoring

Both at trial and hunt we have the situation where two dogs are working the casting line – one must fetch while the other stays and honors.

The honoring dog is usually to the left of the working dog, and in the beginning the handler can fudge: he can get in the way, block the honoring dog's view of the vying dog. Later this is not permitted, but we've got to start somewhere.

Remember our slip lead? Put this on the honoring dog; should he honor, just stand there. After you leave the trial line, congratulate him in no uncertain terms. But while on line you're quiet. That's part of the rules. But should Pup break he'll go only three to five feet and you'll jerk him down good, bring him back to sit in the exact spot he vacated

The advanced honoring dog on the right honors far to front of his handler. He honors the cast of the running dog.

to break, and lean over (in training) and give him a stern lecture. At trial you wouldn't be permitted to have a lead on him, anyway. Once he broke, he'd be gone. Gone from your side and gone from the trial.

Another thing you can do is attach a cord to Pup's welded D-ring on his flat collar and bring that cord across the back of your upper legs and hold it fast with your right hand (if you are a right-handed gunner). Then, when it looks like he's going to break (you're reading Pup all the time), you give the cord a tug – short-circuiting Pup's thinking and getting him to heel, sit, stay.

In the beginning you can even keep the cord taut – Pup knows he's tethered. Later you relax, letting the cord droop, but be ever ready to tighten it should Pup show any indication of going.

Mismarking

A dog that mismarks is usually overexcited or confused. He's just too eager, he's running too fast, he's not concentrating. When he gets to the area of the fall and can't find the bird, he goes berserk and casts away to oblivion or else runs to the bird boy to try to steal a bird lying at his feet.

Once again we must return to the basics, which go like this: You bring Pup to the casting line and tell him to heel, sit, stay. (To help him stay, you can drop your flat palm before his face – same as the traffic cop.) Then you signal for the bird boy to hurrah the bird, making all sorts of noise (or blowing the duck call) and waving the dummy or bird around to hype Pup up. Then he throws the dummy and either fires a training pistol or not. You cast Pup, and he heads to field. Only this time he finds at least a dozen dummies seeded in the area of the fall.

Switching Dummies

But what if Pup picks one dummy up, spits it out, and then goes for another dummy? Well, depending on what age Pup is, you can do one of two things. You can go to field and physically kick the dummy you want Pup to fetch. It will scoot across the ground and excite Pup and he'll leap upon it. Whereupon you tell him "Hold it" and "Heel," and walk him back to the casting line.

If Pup still won't hold, you go to the magic table as explained in chapter 6. (Even though I was talking about bird dogs, the philosophy and technique for the magic table is the same for all species of gun dogs.)

But wait a minute – I said above, ". . . depending on Pup's age." Now this is a tough one. I don't know how precocious your pup is. He may be fired up and savvy, he may be low-keyed and a dullard. He may be mature for his age, he may be immature. That's why you never can say, "Pup should be doing this at such and such an age." Nothing could be more disserving or more incorrect.

Now, I have taken three-month-old pups to the magic table just to prove a point. But that doesn't make the rule, does it? I'd rather Pup be ten months or older before he confronts the magic table. If he's younger than that, all the marking should be taken with a grain of salt, anyway. So he spits out the bird and picks up another; the magic table will eventually deter this. Play another game. Go Happy Timing; lay off the marks until Pup's ready.

But there is another scenario we must discuss. Pup is now eighteen months old and you're throwing him a poor-man's double. That's one bird boy throwing both birds: first from the left; second from the right. Pup can't find the last bird down (generally the one he goes for first), so he runs across field either to try to steal a dummy from the bird boy or to go on past him and pick up the first bird thrown.

This can never be. Why? Well, we're training gun dogs, which means they'll soon be hunting for you. Say you've shot two ducks that landed in the pond. One duck is dead, the other is a strong cripple. Pup dives to retrieve the second bird down (the cripple) and the bird dives on him, so Pup leaves off his hunt and goes for the dead bird. By the time he's brought that bird to hand and returned for the cripple he couldn't find, that bird has swum off to die in the tules. A total waste of game and a denial of the very purpose you took a retriever hunting in the first place: to fetch every bird down.

So Pup can't switch birds.

But let's say he does. He's gone to the last bird down, can't find it, and now starts across field. Several things happen at once. You go nuts (or Pup thinks you do); you come heavy-footed into the field, brandishing the white flyswatter, screaming—all the while the bird boy runs over to get the first bird thrown and hides it behind him so Pup can't find it.

Now you catch Pup and give him the mock-mauling of his life. You chug him and throw him to the ground and straddle his chest and shout down his nose and tell him in no uncertain terms just how displeased you are with him. Then you rise and tell him, "Heel," and walk him back to where he left off his hunt on the second bird thrown. You find the bird (you may need the help of the bird boy) and tell Pup, "Fetch," as you kick the bird with your foot, and Pup leaps for it. Now you tell him, "Heel," and "Hold it," and walk him back to the casting line. Then you run the test again. And again. And again.

There's a rule of dogdom that should be brought to bear here. Any time something bad happens to Pup, he associates the pain or the

displeasure with the place it occurred. You don't go to this place anymore to train. It's that simple – and that complex.

But there's still more you can do. You can heel Pup in the gate of a
fence. Have a bird boy throw one bird north of the fence and the other
bird south of the fence. Should Pup give up his hunt and try to switch
birds, he'll just hit a fence – and you'll be coming running to repeat the
mock-mauling and the procedure explained above. Then you'll have
the bird boy pick up the north bird and run the drill over again.

No-Go or Balking

Now about this time Pup may display another fault. You've intimi-
dated him afield. He's had trouble, and you've brought him back to the
casting line. The bird boy's thrown the double, and you leaned over
and placed your flattened palm next to Pup's face; raising your hand
like you were throwing a bowling ball, you commanded "Back." And
Pup sat there. So you tried a second cast, and Pup still won't go.

Okay, you can put it all away for a few days and let Pup think it
over. But should you bring him to field (a different fence and gate), try
the drill again, and he still refuses to go, then you've got to go to the
chain gang (see chapter 4).

Snap Pup and all the other dogs you can locate to the chain gang
and work another foolproof dog before him: directly before him.
Every once in a while, loft a pigeon to sail right down the line, just
above the dogs' leaping noses. Pup will get the fire stoked up in his
boiler. You'll hear his whistle blowing and see his drivers chugging.
When you let him loose and run him on the drill, no way is he going to
sit there and refuse to cast.

Finally, another way to fire up a reluctant Pup on line is to have a
bird boy cast a cackling cock pheasant from right beside the handler
and have a gunner shoot to kill. This will put a launch in Pup akin to a
Cape Canaveral blast off. To a lesser degree, a female duck *(quack,
quack, quack)* will do the same thing.

But just a minute. This is a great time to explain a truth of gun
dog training. You never solve one problem without creating another.
Right? You tried to break Pup of switching birds, and what was the
result? You got a balker. Then you had to solve the balking problem
before you could go on with the switching problem. That's why we
say, "It's easier to avoid a problem than it is to correct one." But we don't
have that "avoidance" option in this book – all our dogs are problem
dogs. The best we can do, then, is while trying to correct one problem
don't create another. And that's sometimes very hard to do.

Okay, we've corrected the breaker, the no-go, the switcher, and the mismarker. What's left? Plenty. Let's consider the dog who won't wait out a mark.

Refusing to Watch a Mark Down

This problem often comes to front when you've gone to triples or quadruples. That is, there are three or four birds being thrown. Now, of course, we're talking about an older, more seasoned, and wiser dog. Maybe too wise. Here's what he does. You call for the first bird to be thrown; Pup watches the bird boy launch it and the gunner shoot it. But then (Pup is field-wise) he turns his head to watch the number two bird boy and gunner go through their routine – and he never sees the first bird down.

That's right. He did turn his head away. But there is this you must know. Pup has 250 to 270 degrees of vision, whereas we have 180 degrees. In other words, dogs have phenomenal peripheral sight capability. And the truth is, Pup may well have seen the bird down out of the corner of his eye. But it shakes us. How do we know?

Here's what we do.

We stop the whole sequence – right then and there. We yell for the second bird boy not to throw the bird, then lean over and cast Pup for the first fall. Chances are he'll bingo it, but you never know. Henceforth, every time you see Pup turn away from a mark, stop the process and cast him for the bird. Eventually you'll get him to hold his attention.

But you've got to give the old pro his head. I remember Pepe. He knew the bird field by heart. He'd go get the bird he wanted; come back, line himself up, and wait for me to take the bird from his mouth; then cast on his own for the next bird. When all four birds were picked up, he'd return and flip around and wait for me to take the bird. Then he'd have himself lined up for the upcoming blind (to go get the bird he didn't see fall). And 90 percent of the time he was lined up right. That's a remarkable percentage, considering the odds were 250 to one against him (one degree out of 250). But Pepe was just field-wise – he knew what the judges would ask for depending on the way the wind blew, the lay of the land, and where the marks had fallen. Pepe's sister Powder was the same way.

You didn't handle these two retrievers at field or trial. You just stood in awe of their wisdom and took the birds as they came in.

And as with the no-go dog, the use of cackling cock pheasants will more likely see Pup follow the process from hand to ground (or water).

As I've said before, "There's no problem that can't be solved with birds." When all else fails for you, get out the poultry.

Overmarking and Undermarking

It might be a matter of poor depth perception, but some dogs invariably overrun or undershoot a mark. Well, there's a way to help correct this. As the bird's in the air, release Pup for the fetch. He'll run looking at the falling bird and have more chance of gauging its landing.

Of course, you'll later have to stop Pup from breaking. But that's the price we pay for correcting faults: we sometimes create another one.

Also, you can seed the area of the fall, and this will guarantee Pup finds the bird.

Also consider this. It can well be Pup is just too excited and runs zany—he isn't thinking. If that's the case, I recommend a return to heel, sit, and stay interspersed with lots of Happy Timing.

Or I recommend a ton of birds shot for Pup immediately before him. Let him get the hot blood out of his plumbing. Enough birds and he'll start taking them for granted instead of coveting them so bad he runs amuck in searching for them.

Noise on Line

We must recognize that Pup whines on line because he's so hyped up he can't wait to get the bird. There's only one way to break a dog of this. Just tell him, "No noise" each time you finish your trilogy of heel, sit, and stay—and say it so you mean it. Then signal for the bird boy and the gunner to launch a bird and fire. Enough close birds will finally stop Pup from whining on line: *but you will never break him of it.* For the rest of Pup's life you'll have to warn him, "No noise" on the casting line, or noise is what you'll get. Even when he's white-muzzled and stoved up.

If he whimpers in the duck blind, then that's another matter; quite frankly, dogs can tell the difference between hunting and trialing. The judges will throw a vocal dog out of the trial for whimpering, but it may only amuse you on a hunt. Yet, the same dog can whine on hunt and never at a test. You'll see this if you own and run enough retrievers. Also, I've had retriever field-trial champions break on the sound of the safety in a duck blind, but hold fast to even a cock pheasant being launched from line at a trial. The old pros know. They cue from you.

Chewing the Bird or Hard Mouth

Pup's mouth is his front loader, the most important piece of equipment he has for fetching. But several things can go wrong with his mouth: he can chew the bird, he can crush the bird, and he can be sticky mouth (which means he snaps repeatedly at the bird as you're trying to take it).

All these faults will be corrected by the magic table. Just go there and stay there until the job is done. Now we discussed all this in great detail in chapter 6 as we were training bird dogs. If you haven't read that chapter yet, it's imperative you do so now.

But there is this notation. We've seen with retrievers that several dogs on the magic table can be an aid. Dogs are in constant communication with each other, and dogs have a complete spectrum of feelings. Which means they can console each other, or hype each other up; it also means one dog can exhibit jealousy and prod another dog to performance, or another dog can evidence complacency and settle Pup down.

This old thing of dogs communicating came up one morning. My wife told me to get Chili so we could give her some cough syrup. There were five house dogs lying in a clump when I went for Chili—she leaped and ran. But at no time had her name been used—my wife had said, "It's time to give you-know-who her cough medicine." I don't think Chili's that far into deciphering human language. No, she sensed my will for her as I walked toward the pile, and she bolted. Again I stood there stunned. I've seen it happen so many times. And for the life of me I can't understand what the dogs are cuing off. But they are. I used to think it was scent. For, as we think, we stink.

That is, our bodies give different odors to fit our moods. Why else would dogs trigger on butyric acid on a sensitivity scale one million times more acute than man's? For butyric acid is an essential ingredient in sweat, and the average man sweats a quart a day. Also, sweat is heightened by man's stress. Quite easily we can see how Pup would cue off this.

But I can't think I emitted any odor as I walked toward Chili. No, more and more I've got to turn to ESP. And I hate that. It's like a doctor not knowing what's wrong with you, so he says you have a virus. Bosh. Why isn't he honest like I am? Doc hasn't the faintest idea what your problem is, and I haven't the faintest idea of how dogs receive and transmit messages.

And you should know this. The magic table gives us a multiple return on our investment. Not only does it cure sticky mouth, hard mouth, and chewing the bird, but it also bolds the timid pooch up and tames the renegade down. The sequence is this: Pup sees he's pleasing you as he advances on the magic table; you transmit back your pleasure, which he can interpret, which enhances his confidence; and he does even better. Which further compounds your admiration of him, and the circle gets ever wider. As for the renegade dog—he learns you have complete mastery over him, but you don't abuse it. This takes away his fright, should that be his problem. And it smothers his fight, should he just think he's going to be the leader of this dog/man pack. Every dog should be a graduate of the magic table—even those who'll never fetch a thing in their lives. I'd recommend it for all shepherd dogs, guard dogs, sniff dogs, and so forth. Nothing on earth can be better for a dog than the magic table.

Running Away with the Bird

If you're going to see this fault, it will usually be exhibited by a younger dog. Maybe a dog too young to be asked to perform the fetch you've given him. The dog wants to play. He's not had sufficient Happy Timing. And there are several ways to cure this.

Shoot lots of birds for him right off the line. Get him bird sick.

Take him to the magic table.

Return to the power bar.

Happy Time.

Let this dog sleep beside your bed and ride in the cab of your pickup. Make him special. He must come when called. At this time he doesn't see coming as worthwhile.

Any combination of the above will cure him. Just keep tinkering until you find the right combination.

Running out of Control

You'll generally not see a retriever run out of control on a mark or a series of marks. This usually comes up when the dog's been sent for a blind retrieve. Let me explain. You're on a hunt and Pup is afield fetching up a bird while you shoot another one. Pup heard the shot, but he didn't see the bird fly or fall. When he returns to the line with the fetch, you take it from him, and then you line him up and cast him for the "blind." All types of things can go wrong here, and we discuss them later. Pup can refuse the cast, he can take a wrong cast (go the wrong direction), or he can take the cast and go to field but not answer your whistle and hand signals as you try to whistle him down and head him for the fall. And then, if there have been too many trainer mistakes made with Pup in teaching blind retrieves, he can eventually doff his cap and say, "See ya," and bolt off cross country.

Everything is wrong with this Pup. So he must be taken back to basics: he needs review of the power bar, the magic table, the chain gang—the whole bit. You've got to get this Pup in pocket or he'll be worthless to you the rest of his life.

One thing's certain: Pup's uncertain. So you've got to build his confidence. That's done with all three of our aids: power bar, magic table, and chain gang.

Also, Pup has no idea of what whistle and hand signals mean, so he'll have to be taken back through the baseball diamond drill. (I know we haven't had that, but it'll come up soon.)

So to that end we'll move along. First, we'll have a chapter on water problems; then we'll go to handling. Okay?

10

Water

IN 1933, WHEN I was four years old, my family didn't have a swimming pool. We didn't even have a bathtub; we all bathed in the kitchen sink. It fell one night with Dad in it, and he broke all his ribs on his right side as he scraped down the wall and hit the plumbing. My point is, there are hazards with water.

But I was speaking of swimming pools. South of my hometown of Wichita, Kansas, there was a concrete pool with a house where you could change clothes. The place was called Park-of-Fun. I'll never forget that water. It was a bilious green, like an olive with a light bulb in it. And there'd be tadpoles and frogs, and an occasional snake to glide, splash, or plop in that water. It took all my courage to jump in, and when I did I thought I'd just tipped a kayak on a walrus hunt, for surely there were icebergs feeding that water.

Now I don't care if retrievers do have webbed feet – they, too, can have misgivings around water. It all depends on how they're started. We call it water love. Did you start the pup so he had water love? You can do that, you know. Run Pup in a pack on a hot day. Get all the dogs panting good, then head for the farm pond where they all jump in and lap and twirl and splash about. In that one episode you cured Pup of most water problems for life.

But things don't always work out that way. And when they don't, you've got trouble. Like the man said, "Right here in River City."

Introducing Pup to Water Marks

Walk Pup out on a peninsula. Have a bird boy sit in a boat or stand (wearing waders) in shallow water. Give the signal and have the boy throw a boat bumper so it's straight out from the line of the peninsula. Cast Pup and he'll go make the fetch. The point being – he'll cast, rather than try to run a bank, for there is no bank to run.

Consider starting Pup from a straight bank. The bird boy throws the bird, and Pup runs down the bank to leap in – reducing the distance he must go by water before making his retrieve. That's fine with me if you're hunting Pup. But he'll be out of a trial if you're campaigning him. Understand? Water tests at field trials or test hunts must be conducted by water – never by land. Land is the hazard, land is the test. Touch land and you've failed the test. It's that simple, and it's that incredible to Pup who, webbed feet or not, finds his natural element ashore. He's a Marine: by land, sea, or air. But he's going to stay dry as long as he can – and if he must get wet, he's going to get out of the water as quick as possible.

So in the beginning, all water marks are offered to Pup off the end of peninsulas: singles, doubles, and triples if possible. Also it's imperative that no matter where the dummy lands, the spot where you're

A perfect first-time water mark for Pup includes the following: bird boy on far shore; Pup and handler on peninsula; dummy landing on water where closest landfall is peninsula he cast from. There is also no debris in water: Pup has a clear mark. And there is no decisive wind to move water.

standing is the nearest dry dock. Let me explain. If the dummy landed by a far shore, Pup would be unduly tempted to make for that landfall. And he would be wrong. For the rule in test hunts is that judges want to see Pup come back the way he went out. And we have a way to teach that. It's called the looking glass drill, and we'll discuss that when we're dealing with faults on running blind retrieves.

No-Go

But let's say Pup just won't cast to water. Well, we've got a real problem, folks, and once again we solve it by returning to basics. Take Pup Happy Timing with a pack, and get them hot and walk to shore. Pup may enter water or not. If he doesn't, then you go to water. Go there in waders or in a boat or in a bathing suit, but go. And take some tidbits with you. Toss one ashore. Let Pup eat it. Now toss one halfway between you and Pup so it lands in the water. Keep coaxing Pup out. If he won't come, then cut out his feeding for a couple or three days.

Or, take Pup to sea in a boat and have children tag along in life vests to entice Pup to enter the water and play with them. If necessary, slide Pup in. No, I didn't say throw him; I said to pick him up and gently slide him in. He'll turn around and paddle back as quick as he can. Pull him aboard and give him a treat, tell him what a great guy he is, then put him in the water again.

Incidentally, you help Pup get in a boat one of two ways. First, you grab the hair on each side of his neck and pull him aboard; second, if possible, let him get his forearms over the gunwales, then push down on the back of his neck so he plops over into the boat.

If you still can't get Pup to cast to water, then put Pup on a short lead and walk him to water, ever coaxing him along by playing with a dummy that you toss straight up in the hope Pup will frolic with you. Carry treats. Give them often. Praise Pup.

Henceforth, when you go to the peninsula to cast Pup for a mark the bird boy has thrown, do not stand on shore. Instead, walk Pup out a few feet into the water so he's already wet. A wet Pup will be more likely to cast to water than one standing dry.

If none of this works, put your chain gang right along shore and shoot birds before the lot. Have a helper release the dog you want sent for the fetch. Or join a gun dog club and have all the members stand with their dogs along the shore – the dogs will all honor; that is, they'll stay while another dog works. Then you have a bird boy and gunner work the bird, and you repeatedly cast Pup for the fetch. Oh, he'll love it – seeing all the other dogs pleading to be let loose so they can go make the fetch. Remember, nothing trains a dog like other dogs. It's your responsibility to think up ways this can be done for each problem you face.

Running the Bank

Well, you can't hunt or trial the world from the end of a peninsula. Things just don't work out like that. Eventually you've got to go to a regular straight shoreline. And when you do, let's hope Pup won't try to run the bank. For bank running is very hard to correct. Some of the best pros in the business have failed – and some have nearly killed a dog in doing it. They put an electric collar on the dog and shock him if he doesn't hit the water. They hide helpers in the bushes with whips to jump out and beat Pup to water. They reach down and pick up a shotgun and shoot Pup with bird shot if he shies from water and runs the bank.

But not us.

The primary thing we do is run Pup on the looking glass drill, which I'm still not ready to show you. See the section on running a straight line in chapter 12.

We simply run Pup from water. We continue to walk him into the water, tell him to heel, sit, and stay, and signal for the bird boy to throw the bird.

You can wear your slip lead. Tie one end to your belt, thread the other end through Pup's D-ring, and hold this end of the cord in your right hand (if you're a right-handed gunner). Should Pup head to sea when you cast him, just let the loose end of the slip lead go and Pup easily slips away. But should he try to double back and run the bank, then let him hit the end of the double-backed cord and jerk him down good. Then line him up again with heel, sit, stay, and cast him. He'll eventually go.

About this lining up. This would all have been covered in basic retrieving, but that's not what this book's about. We've got a problem-solving book. But let's review the set-up of a dog on line, anyway.

Setting a dog up is a process. You can either pat your right outside leg and get Pup to cross before your body (he's naturally heeling to your left-hand side if you're a right-handed gunner), or coax him with your palm to go on around you, then pat your left leg, stop him with his ears at your pants seam, and tell him to heel, sit, stay.

What we're looking for is this: We want to be able to lean back and look down Pup's spine and make certain it's pointing in the direction the gunner and bird boy stand or to that spot where you figure the bird will land. In other words, Pup's lined up. And that's why we call it "lining a blind" when we get to blind retrieving.

When Pup's gone afield to get a bird and he's coming back, you have your left leg extended for him to go about your body and ease up to it – all in line with the direction of the fall of the second bird to be fetched. Once again, you check the spine. It should point straight to the bird. If not, then re-heel Pup. Carousel him about you or use hand signals to get him to scoot about beside you and get situated.

When you cast Pup, make a weather vane of your body by extending your left leg and left arm, laying the flat of your palm immediately beside Pup's head. Mesmerize him by slowly revolving your palm until you see the shutter snap. That is, Pup will tell you when he has the picture you want him to see. He'll rise up slightly, his pelvic drive muscles will grow tense, his eyes will sharpen, the crimp in his ears will rise and lay parallel with the earth. He's ready to go. So you cast him with a great boom of voice, "Back," as you slice your hand up like you were throwing a bowling ball. You've launched Pup, he's on his way with momentum. Which is especially needed around water.

But back to bank running. You can run Pup out of a fake duck blind where there's a hole cut so he can stick his head out. He sees the bird boy throw and the gunner shoot and the duck splash. You yell, "Back," and he leaps from the blind to water. Which means he's already gotten wet. So there's no need cheating back to dry land. It's getting the dog wet that's the test of the thing.

You also can position Pup by hemming him in. For example, you're to his right and there's a great cut bank (or a thorn bush or thick stand of reeds) to his left. When you say, "Back," he has nowhere to go but to sea unless he turns himself inside out to go backwards – which is not likely.

Heading for Another Shore

In the beginning, you must always make sure the place you stand is the nearest landfall. If not, you'll find Pup scooping up the bird and heading for a near shore – which is not your shore. And this can never be. For Pup must come in as he went out. I'll never forget Happy: he was a British retriever in my kennel. I once cast him for a duck while gunning at Cheyenne Bottoms in central Kansas. The duck, unfortunately, was head shot and glided for a far shore. Happy was not a reluctant water dog – he had enough water love – but still, if there was a shorter way back by land, he'd prefer to take it. Well, he did. And that really turned into a mess. For the far shore was a dike, and the dike had a road on it, and Happy got on that road and ran away. It was that simple. He kept thinking he was heading for the blind, but the road bent away. And the blind ended up south, the road angling off north. And the more Happy tried to get to the blind, the farther away he got. Finally I had to go get him. Which shows the problem you can get into if a dog favors going to a shore that is far from you but near to him.

Then too, I had a friend whose prized retriever disappeared into the tules on a water blind. In actuality, he was on a far shore. And it took my friend a month to get his dog back. The dog was eventually found with a man who claimed mistaken identity — he thought this prized Lab was his run-of-the-mill mutt. "I swear it," he said.

Well, if Pup is going to head for another shore, then you must emerge from your duck blind and get on the whistle and shout and wave your arms and look delirious. Which you are. Or should be.

And since we didn't have basics on whistle and hand signals, now is a good time to look at those. One long blast on the whistle means sit, one semi-long blast and a series of short tweets means to come in. You blow the sit whistle, Pup complies; then you wait for him to compose himself, and you give him one of four arm signals. You walk to either side with an arm up (to the left with the left arm up; to the right with the right arm up) and that means to go either left or right. You take a step forward with your arm raised and that means get on back farther. Or you lean over at the waist while you blow the come-in whistle, and you coax Pup to you by continually raising and dropping your right arm (your left arm if you're holding a gun). Now, when you move sideways you accompany this body-and-hand signal with the oral command "Over." When you step forward with your hand upraised you say, "Back." But you do not say come in. No, the whistle does that for you: the *toooooooot, tweet, tweet, tweet*. All done in a trill. And done over and over again. Continually bending your body at your waist, dropping your non-gun hand, and milking Pup in like you were retrieving a rope with one hand. Raising and alternately dropping the hand over and over.

But back to heading for a far shore.

If you see Pup mismark and go on toward a far shore, then get on the sit whistle fast. Even yell, "Hey, Pup, Heeeeeeel. You hear me? Heel." You've got to keep him from touching the far shore — with or without the dummy.

Also, when you see Pup fetch the dummy up, get on the come-in whistle immediately. Don't let Pup even think of going anywhere else but to you. And if he does go the wrong way, shout, "No, no, no!" And I mean shout it like a marine drill instructor. Really boom it out. You want to short-circuit Pup's thinking and prompt him to mend his ways. Remember, you and Pup are a team. You must know the hazards that face him. You must know the mistakes he's likely to make. And you must be ready. You must help him. If you're just dawdling, talking to your hunting buddy, not paying any attention, there's no telling where Pup will end up. It's up to you. Many dog mistakes are man mistakes. Remember that. Realize that. Avoid that.

Spitting the Duck Out

Most dogs will shake the minute their bodies clear water. Be ready. Yell "No," or get on the come-in whistle, or get out of the duck blind and go confront Pup at water's edge. Many trainers try to stop the dog from shaking. And it can be done. But I'm not talking about a two-year-old Pup. I'm talking about a seasoned performer. All that's important to you is if Pup does shake (and he will) that he doesn't drop the bird. It just makes sense. Pup's on this hunt for three reasons. First, for the love of him, the way he makes ordinary events memorable; second, he keeps you from having to swim for the duck; and third, he conserves game. But let's say he's got a strong cripple in his mouth, or a duck that revived en route from the water, and Pup drops it only to have the duck *quack* and fly away. Now you've let a wounded duck go to die in the tules somewhere and be eaten by crows. Is that what you had in mind? I don't think so. You wanted that duck for yourself. And the law of nature demands you have it. Otherwise, you've senselessly killed a bird, and there's no excuse for that.

If Pup won't hold the duck and deliver to hand, you know what you've got to do. Go to the magic table. Now this was all discussed in chapter 6. Turn there now and get that technique down pat. Then run Pup through the fetch drill until he's foolproof. No longer will he spit the bird out.

Leaving a Diving Cripple

Most dogs won't switch birds in the water. It's too much effort. Where they could easily do so with land beneath their feet, it takes a lot of energy and determination to swim across a pond for a second fetch. Most dogs will stay in the area of the fall, yet some will become discouraged (or confused) if a duck keeps diving on them.

Sure, some dogs will dive right after them, but not all will. Most will try to stand up in the water to better bend their necks and look

This young Chesie pup is shown the difference between his custom-made dummy and a beached decoy.

down – trying to see the duck. But then the duck plops up some twenty feet to side. And by the time Pup's gotten over there, the duck's dived again.

Well, it doesn't take much smarts to build yourself a device that similates this in the water. Just run a long cord to a dummy secured with a clothespin, then bring the line under a rod that's moored in the pond's bottom. When the dog is ready to pluck up the dummy, you pull the line and the dummy dives. Should Pup wait it out, he'll eventually grab the dummy. *Eureka!* Nothing succeeds like success. Having won one, Pup'll more than likely bide his time when he confronts the real diving duck.

But there is nothing like having your dog with you all the time to get him savvy to all sorts of things that can happen to him on an actual hunt. I'll explain. Danny Duff, of Carbondale, Colorado, and I were fly-fishing the Roaring Fork River, and we had Danny's neat little bitch Coley along. Well, Coley was running up and down the bank, retrieving tree limbs and whatever else she could find, when she suddenly spotted a snag bobbing up and down in the roaring current.

To get to the snag she had to gauge her route, entering the water some thirty feet up shore. Then, angling to the snag, she grabbed out at it with her mouth as she went by. Well, she grabbed the protruding snag (finally) only to have it bend down and go under water (it was secured to a sunken tree trunk). Coley went down with it. Undaunted, she came up and let go to float downstream as she paddled for shore. Then she ran the bank and gave it another try – and another and another. You think this self-discovered drill won't help her when she confronts a diving duck? Folks, that duck's in the bag!

It's always this way. There's just no substitute for living with your dog. Taking him everywhere you go, including him in all your projects, never leaving him at home even when he has to stay tied up at camp while you're hunting elk, turkey, or antelope. Being tied up will even teach him patience and how to combat a boring day.

Retrieving Decoys

A dog will retrieve decoys – some dog that's just never been exposed to training-as-you-hunt so he could hunt as you trained. Of course, decoys are enticing: floating out there, bobbing up and down. After all, they do look alive; that's why they serve as decoys. So the poor hapless Pup that's never been exposed to them in training just naturally wants to go investigate them when cast to sea – and possibly drag them back to shore.

The way to take a pup off decoys is to bring the decoys ashore. Scatter them around in a circle and heel Pup through them, telling him "No" when he gets too interested in any one decoy. Then later, you toss dummies into the layout of decoys and have Pup run in there – on dry land – and fetch the dummies up.

Same goes for learning how to handle a boat. The boat is always dragged ashore. Then Pup is worked out of the boat in dry dock. This is especially important when using a skiff or a pirogue. These boats tip easily and both hunter and dog must learn how to counterbalance each other. As Pup places his forelegs over the gunwales, you, the handler, lean the opposite way to counterbalance Pup's weight. Then, as Pup comes aboard, bring your own weight back to center. It's done as a team – as is all dog training. If you'll get the hang of it on dry land, you'll never get wet asea.

Retrieving from a Dog Box

Same goes with a dog box. This is a box built to proportion to house

Pup on a day's hunt, or a ride in the car, or a night in a motel. On one end, there is a great U cut out so Pup can stick his neck out and see what's going on. At the bottom of the U there's a big O-bolt where the D-ring of Pup's flat collar is swivel-snapped.

The sequence of introducing Pup to the dog box will usually go like this. Pup will not want to get into the box. He won't want to stay snapped. When he does go get a bird, he'll bring it back, but he'll not want to get back in the box. Eventually, after enough birds are shot over Pup, he'll come back and leap in the box to twist about and be ready for the next flight. At that point, it's time to leave off the hunt, you'll have to pull him from the box, for he won't want to go.

As always, we bring the dog box to dry land and throw out dummies to earth in training. Remember, it's always easier to work things out ashore than it ever could be on water.

Going to Land

If you have a dog that's constantly going to the nearest land with his fetch, then you've got to break him of it. The dog has to come back as he went out – and for sure we didn't let him run the bank to be nearer the floating bird and then dive in.

But you'll see this. I'm not talking about going to a far shore that's nearer to Pup. I'm talking about going to land – especially as Pup is making his way to the duck. What if the duck were thrown on the far side of a figure-eight-shaped pond with a slot through the center two circles? Or a peninsula is sticking out and is tempting Pup to dry-dock either on his way to the bird or coming back? Usually, the problem shows itself when Pup has gone to get a bird that was close to shore – say, thirty feet down from you. And it just makes good sense that rather than swim thirty feet to come back, Pup just turns and goes ten feet (let's say) to reach shore. Then Pup will run the shoreline back to you and hand over the bird. Well, this can't be. It's a smart way to hunt, but you can't ever place in a trial or hunt test with such a performance.

So what do we do?

First off, we cast all our retrieves straight out – we don't angle them from shore. We just never give this dog a chance to dry-dock anywhere except before the casting line.

But, of course, later in training we've got to start with the angles, and we do it gradually. You can tell what Pup's going to do. If you see him head for shore while going to fetch a bird, or having the bird in mouth, turn and head for the near bank, you yell, "No!" And you yell it good. If you must, enter the water. Leave the casting line and walk forward directly into the water, all the time giving Pup the come-in whistle and clapping your hands and encouraging him by voice to come directly to you instead of angling for a bank.

If necessary, run him with a long trailing check cord and physically bring him back. But be careful, this can frighten a dog. Do it easily, never pulling so hard as to cause Pup to want to rear back.

Let's say Pup heads for shore on his way to a bird. Have the bird boy walk forward and fire the gun directly into the water. We call this "sluicing." And it works like magic in getting Pup's attention and hyping him up to make the retrieve. Of course, you can't do this if Pup has the bird in his mouth and is going to shore on his retrieve.

Use your own judgment. You can whistle and display and shout for Pup to come to you. Or you can sluice the water before you with a live shell or popper shot. A popper is a blank shotgun shell that has enough power to blow the plug out and make a splash in water.

In other words, gunshots and splashes excite Pup and tend to make him go in that direction.

If all else fails, then just return Pup to making all his water retrieves from the end of the peninsula, which will be the nearest landfall Pup can make, no matter where the dummy (or bird) lands.

Conclusion

That's about it for water marks. This really is the simplest of our water problems. Where things get tough is when we ask Pup to fetch a bird up he hasn't seen fall. In other words, running a water blind. First, we'll go to land blinds, for that's where we teach whistle and hand signals. Eventually we'll go to water. There are a thousand hazards out there to plague us, and we'll learn how to avoid them.

11

Land Blinds

EVER TRY TO thread a needle? Could you hit the hole? No? Why? I see, there were hazards. Lint stuck out and caught the sides of the hole, and you couldn't get the thread through. So you slicked it with spit and twisted it to a point and tried again. But to no avail? Yes, the tip bent and jammed and kept the thread from going through.

Well, it seems to me you've got the same problems here that you find when you try to teach a dog to line. To thread the needle, if you please. The object is to have Pup go to field to find a bird he hasn't seen fall. He does it with a deliberate, aiming cast, as well as being stopped afield and given whistle, oral, and body signals until he finally arrives at the hidden bird.

There are many ways to teach lining, but they're all based on a pattern drill. Personally, I know of none better than the simple baseball diamond.

Let's run through it.

Grab a handful of dummies and walk Pup out to the pitcher's mound. Tell Pup to heel, sit, and stay while you toss three dummies to first base, turn and toss three dummies to second base, and turn and toss three dummies to third base. Then heel Pup to home plate, turn him around, and tell him to heel, sit, and stay.

Professional handler Danny Duff prepares to cast a Lab by holding his hand directly above *the dog's head.*

Hunting retriever club enthusiast Dan Sullivan casts his dog by placing his hand immediately beside *the dog's head.*

Now line up Pup. That is, lean back and make certain his spine is pointing in the direction you're going to cast him. If you want him to go to first base, he should be angled right. Now tell him, "Line, line, line," with a low, provocative voice, making it all mysterious and serious. When you see Pup focus—and you will—then cast him for the blind.

This handler works Pup on a baseball diamond drill using a mowed playground in a residential subdivision. These are excellent conditions with which to start this drill.

This handler lets his dog orient in a typical tall-grass pasture. Many dummies are used so Pup has good sighting for fetch.

The handler has stopped Pup at the pitcher's mound and given him a right-hand over for retrieve.

And how do you tell if he's in focus? His pelvic drive muscles will tense, he'll raise up, his eyes will sharpen, his head will extend, and his ears will cock so the bend of them is parallel with the earth. And what are you doing to get this behavior? You're standing to the right side of Pup (if you're a right-handed gunner) and you have your left arm beside his upper body. Your left hand is made into a knife, and that hand is beside Pup's head (some want the hand over the head and between the eyes), and you slowly rotate the hand – mesmerizing Pup to focus.

When Pup's got the picture, you cast him by lifting your left hand up as though you were throwing a bowling ball and commanding, "Back." Pup will scoot out and fetch up the first-base dummy.

Now cast him to second base.

Then to third base.

Do it over and over, selecting the bases at random. This finished, put Pup away for the day and try him later in the week. Finally, take Pup to the pitcher's mound and throw out your dummies to each of the bases, then heel Pup to home plate. Cast him for second base, but hit him with the sit whistle (one long blast). Pup will turn and sit and look at you for hand and oral directions. Now, walk to your right, with your right arm extended and raised, and say, "Over." Say it in low voice. Saying it loud can push Pup back – away from his line to first base. To counteract this, some handlers give the *over* signal with body and hand and say nothing. Others give the *over* signal with body and hand while blowing the come-in whistle at the same time. For realize this: the natural tendency of Pup always will be to go back, not to the side. And there will be many hazards to reinforce this.

For example, when running up a slope, Pup will fall off. Or when running with a cross wind, Pup will be blown away – he'll fall off to the force of it. Or he'll bend to, or away, from cover. There are a thousand things that can suck him off line.

But let's say Pup refuses to take an *over*.

Refusing to Take a Hand Signal

Okay, he's hung up at the pitcher's mound and won't take the *over* to first base. You try to coax him over there, and he does one of several things: he turns and tries to run to second base; he tries to come in; or he just lies down in rebellion or confusion. Pick up a dummy and toss it to first base. Now he has a mark there to retrieve. Tell him, "Over," and he'll cast there. Now give him the come-in whistle so he'll return to home plate. I'll repeat: the come-in whistle is a medium-long blast followed by a series of tweets. Over and over. Also, the handler bends over at the waist and uses his non-gun hand to milk Pup in. That is, the hand is raised and lowered as though the man were grasping, pulling, and releasing a rope.

Now cast Pup back for second base. Hit him with the sit whistle at the pitcher's mound. Then give him an *over* to first. He'll undoubtedly take it. But he may be unsure of himself. So you start walking toward first base, continually giving your right-hand cast. Or you walk straight toward the pitcher's mound giving the right-hand cast. One way or the other will coax Pup to finally take the cast and go to first base.

Now you've got to do it all over again for third base.

Then you've got to do it for second base. Here's how. Whistle Pup down as he passes the pitcher's mound, and have him sit and look to you for directions. Then, step forward with your hand raised like a traffic cop and cast that hand directly forward as you command, "Back."

Pup'll spin and run on to second base to make his retrieve.

But let's say Pup refuses to take an *over* to either side – nor will he take a *back*, nor will he come in. He's just flat confused and doesn't have the slightest idea what he's supposed to do. Okay, it's back to the power bar. You step off and blow the come-in whistle. You stop and blow the sit whistle. No longer do you tell him to heel, sit, stay. You do it all by whistle until Pup's fail-safe.

Then you check-cord him afield, having him lace the field before you. When he reaches the right-hand cast, blow your sit whistle and have your left arm extended as you walk that way. When Pup hits the left-hand end of his cast, you blow the sit whistle; having your right arm extended you walk right, pulling Pup (if necessary) to have him go that way. Note: Pup does not sit here, you just cause him to stop and pay attention to take directions with the sit whistle.

So the power bar will teach Pup to stop and come in. Remember our come-in drill? I described it in part one, on bird dogs – that's why I tell you it is necessary to read the whole book. You walk before a seated Pup and drop the power bar to wedge into the earth. It now jams between the dirt and Pup's D-ring on his flat collar. He can't rise and move forward. When you want him to come, you flip the bar up and milk it in fast as you give the come-in whistle.

Okay, Pup's going back and coming in with the power bar. And we've got him taking left- and right-hand signals with the check cord while he quarters the field. There is no more. That's it. Now take him back to the ball diamond when you're sure he's ready.

Refusing to Answer a Whistle

See the discussion above on refusing to take a hand signal. It's all applicable.

Refusing to Fetch the Bird

Go back to the magic table in chapter 6.

Unable to Handle Cover

If Pup had sufficient Happy Timing his world would have disappeared. Let me explain that. Cover is stopping him from fulfilling his retrieve. It bothers him, it worries him, it hurts him. But if he'd had lots of Happy Timing with the pack, he'd have learned to barge right through ice on a pond, multiflora rose thickets that prick, hedgerows that stab, hills that slope, winds that blow him off course, and ditches that cause him to emerge off line.

Let me explain that last situation. Each dog has a prominent lead foot. Some have a right-foot lead, others, a left-foot lead. So Pup's sent to fetch a blind where he must run through a ditch or jump a ditch. If he jumps, he'll come down on his lead foot. If that's his left foot, then the right foot will cross over and Pup will dip toward the left. And vice versa. As a result, many ditch crossings are necessary to get Pup to compensate so he'll hold the same line leaving the ditch that he had entering it.

Also, all life takes the path of least resistance. If there's a road running parallel to the line to the blind where the cover is not high, Pup will be tempted to swerve to the road. Only the road curves away from Pup's goal. Now he's off line. And it'll be hard to bring him back to the heavy cover to run the straight line. Try to avoid easy paths at all costs.

Same goes for a pile of bramble in direct route to the blind. Pup will want to swerve around this pile, which will head him off course. Well, this can't be. He must be stopped and driven over the pile. And know this: it's much easier to get Pup to take a *back* than it is an *over.* An *over* tells him he's off line. It tells him he has already failed. Pup doesn't want to fail, so he'll be reluctant to take your *over.* He'll be reluctant to admit to you that you're right and he's wrong. But a *back* tells Pup he's going in the right direction. You just confirmed it. That's why some handlers never give an *over;* instead, they give what's called an *angled back.*

They don't step parallel with the casting line. They step forward at a forty-five-degree angle, casting their arm the same way, saying "Back." This means they stop Pup short of being in line with the bird where he could have taken a direct *over.* Now he's stopped long before the bird and given an *angled back* so the angle will drift him to the bird.

Problems with Cold Land Blinds

A cold land blind has nothing to do with temperature but everything to do with how the bird was set up. If Pup had just run a triple mark and delivered the third bird to hand, and you turned him around and put your hand down beside his head and told him, "Line," he can live with that. He just found three birds out there — why can't there be a fourth? So he casts. And you handle him to the bird.

Or, let's say Pup walks to the casting line (or into the bird field or the duck blind), and a distant shot is heard. That, too, makes for a "hot" blind. Pup heard the shot; it's feasible there's a bird out there to retrieve.

But the cold land blind offers no inducements. You just walk Pup to the line, have him look out to a blank field, and cast him for a bird.

This can come up on an actual day's hunt, let alone a contrived field trial. You've just finished the day and are coming in when you pass a blind where the occupant asks, "Hey, mister, would you send your dog for a duck I shot? I know he's dead, but my dog won't go get it."

So you lay down your gear, heel Pup in the general direction the guy has told you, and cast Pup for the retrieve.

This, then, is the hardest of all retrieves to make. Pup must have absolute trust in you. For he's running "blind" with no inducement to self-propel. All the propulsion must come from you, the handler.

And many dogs balk.

Well, you've just got a case here of not enough "hot" blinds. Pup's not yet got his confidence. So the remedy is simple. Keep running every kind of drill you can think of. Bring Pup to the line and tell him, "Back." But say Pup refuses. Okay. Toss a dummy out there and cast him: he'll find two. So now when he returns with the thrown bird, cast him for the planted bird.

Hunting club enthusiast Hars Haugen runs his flat-coated retriever through a line drill. This drill proves to Pup that there's always a bird or a dummy out there whenever you cast him.

Or run a line of dummies across the field—all so Pup can see them. You bring him to the line cold and tell him, "Back." But this time he can look out there and see a dummy. You cast him and he finishes his retrieve. Then on the same line you cast him again. He goes another ten yards farther and makes his retrieve. Keep this up until he's going 100 yards.

On the next dash, don't plant the short retrieves, just plant a pile at 100 yards. Cast Pup and he'll go. If not, then cast him and walk a ways with him, continually telling him "Back" and throwing forward your upraised arm.

Or, plant a pile of dummies along a brick wall or a chain-link fence. Tell Pup "Back," and he'll be more inclined to run the route laid out by the wall.

Some trainers will mow a path and lay out dummies along it so Pup can make ever longer, repeated retrieves. But I gave that up. It's just too dangerous to have Pup running a path of least resistance on a blind.

Another thing I've done, successfully, is get Pup in the pickup and drive along dropping dummies in a large, flat field. Drive in a straight line and let Pup see each dummy dropped. Then stop the truck, get out, and cast him for the lineup—one at a time.

Anyway, after all this, Pup will eventually run a cold land blind. And this is imperative. For the toughest job Pup can ever draw is to be sent for a cold water blind. Prepare him on land for a blind coming up that's filled with hazards.

The Pop

No, I ain't talking about a bottle of soda. Pup pops when he's running out from you on a cast but suddenly decides he doesn't know what he's doing. So, he stops and turns around for help. Oh, misery of miseries. This is the worst of them all.

Take him back through all the simple baseball diamond drills, and the dummies-in-line drills. You've got to make him a sure performer; you've got to give him faith in himself.

If Pup still pops, don't ever help him. That's the worst thing you can do. Pup failed, so he turned for help, and you forgave him and extended a helping hand. Well, you just wiped out whatever self-assurance we were trying to build. Now Pup knows any time the going gets rough, he can depend on you for help.

So when Pup pops, turn your back on him. It's that simple. And since you know you have a popping dog, and you know a pop is

Handler and dog are surrounded by a wagon wheel of dummies. This drill teaches fine-line discrimination. When you get thirty-six dummies laid around, Pup must really split the eye of the needle to win. This drill cuts down on Pup's popping on fetch, for once again, he's assured there's a dummy out there every time he's cast.

certain, you have a helper off a ways facing Pup. So long as Pup looks at you for help, keep your back turned on him. But the split second he moves and shows some self-initiative, the helper will signal you, and you'll turn to face Pup and give him a solid sit whistle. Which means, you'll handle him if he's moving on his own, but never if he's idle and waiting for you. It may take months of this, but Pup will eventually get the confidence it takes to run a blind and not pop.

That's it for land blinds. They are, in the great scope of retrieverdom, relatively simple. But not water blinds. They are the nemesis of all dogs. In the old-time classic retriever-trial format, the water blind was usually the last test of the day. By that time there might only be eight dogs called back out of a starting entry of eighty. It was the test to guarantee separation so the dogs could place themselves and the judge not be criticized; I mean it's self-evident to everyone whether or not the dog lined the blind. Now, let me explain that term. The ideal is to cast the dog and have him run (or swim) a straight line to and from the planted bird with no whistle, oral command, or hand cast from the handler. The dog lined the blind. He got it on his own.

The water blind is the supreme separator of a dog's performance at trial or afield. And the cold water blind is a test devised in hell to torment both dog and handler. We'll deal with it all in the next chapter.

12

Water Blinds

WE'VE NOTED WATER'S not Pup's natural element, even if he does have webbed feet. Oh, he'll go frolicking with you on a warm summer day, and he'll trout fish with you (by trying to fetch the fish). But that's fun. Come winter—when the ice is on the pond and the brush is buried in snow and a great northern is blowing down and lapping the open part of the pond to white caps—Pup would just as soon be home in front of the fireplace.

And yet you want him to go get a bird he's not seen fall. And he's got to get it with no prior encouragement (such as a gunshot or having just returned from retrieving marks). Well, that's where we separate the immortals from the also-rans.

Realize that all basic training for water is always done on land. And we've done that. We've run the baseball diamond drill and the line drills. Pup knows his whistle, oral, and hand signals. And he knows what a blind retrieve is: he's run hundreds on land. But here on water there poses one pivotal difference.

We never cast Pup for the poultry on a water blind; instead, we always cast him away from the hazards. The handler's goal is not to get the bird, but to avoid the hazards. Yet the great handlers can make it look like they were going for the bird all along.

Dan Sullivan gives Pup back in water, a cast to left, and a cast to right.

Going to Land

The paramount hazard to a water blind is, of course, land. Pup's supposed to get wet, go wet, and stay wet – then make his retrieve and come back wet. Then he's to hold the bird while he shakes and delivers to hand. To fail in any sequence is to fail the test. And to fail any sequence while running a cold water blind while hunting may see Pup lost in the tules, maybe never to be found.

There are two classic land hazards that most judges employ to trip up Pup. One is the figure eight pond where there's a water gap between the two circles. Pup is to thread his way through the hourglass of the figure eight and go into the top pond – never touching land. But land is gaping out, it's reaching out, it's begging Pup – especially a cold Pup – to come ashore. It has all the seduction of those old sirens who used to pose on the rocks and serenade sailors to crash their boats ashore.

The other hazard is to have Pup skim past a peninsula. That is, if Pup does swim a straight line from the casting line to the planted bird (these birds are sometimes held in place with weighted line and clothespins), then his shoulder must just skim the end of the peninsula.

And there's another hazard just as bad: that's an acute angle blind to the bird where Pup is run down a shoreline at a fifteen-degree angle (let's say). That is, the bird is fifty yards distant and fifteen degrees from shore. Which means, you heel Pup around so he's facing down the bank – wow, what a temptation to run the bank. But we can't run the bank, can we? That's the rule. So Pup's either got to run that fifteen-degree line and hit the water going that critical way, or else you've got to heel him about, plunge him ninety degrees straight into the water, and then give a fifty-yard *over*.

In every instance, land is the hazard.

And then, finally, there's the reverse of it all: the defiance of all that we've taught that can come up at trial or afield. That's when Pup must go to shore to make the retrieve. I'll show you how.

We're hunting a relatively large pond that has a dike or an elevated footpath running straight through the center of it. Now the bird's planted in the far pond. To get Pup to fetch that bird, he must go to land. He must emerge from water, run across the dike, and dive back in. And yet, we've spent months driving Pup from land, whistling and yelling and waving our arms about and jumping up and down and praying and cursing and thinking seriously about taking up golf.

So that's the paradox. That's the can of worms. Which means this: Pup must become a master journeyman. He must have some innate sense as to when to touch shore and when to avoid it like the plague. That's the dog we all want. There's the other dog – the mechanical dog – that just hands his will totally over to man and does exactly what he's told. But this dog has a problem. Robbed of his individual initiative, when this dog is out of sight and realizes his handler is not available to help him, he goes berserk.

The mechanical dog runs as a robot, his self-will beaten or burned or shot out of him. He cannot take the initiative because that's always been denied him. All he can do is respond to the handler's signals – and they may not always be right.

The journeyman dog, however, has been brought along to enhance all his God-given senses and innate genius. The dog can think on his own, can use his own good judgment. He can turn off the handler and take over – and be right.

I'll give you an example told to me by Omar Driskill, a professional hunting retriever trainer from Simsboro, Louisiana, while we sat on his front porch drinking iced tea and watching the rain fall. "Bill," he said, "I was in a duck blind and I knocked down a couple of ducks to the right. It was a high wind. And then I knocked down a real long sailer that was about 250 yards over to my left.

"Well, I went ahead and picked up my ducks out front, and I came in and wanted to line towards this X – this imaginary spot X – where I saw that long-sailing duck go down.

"So, I lined the dog out of there, and about 150 yards out he just suddenly took off to the right. I blew my whistle and he refused to heed it. This particular dog was trained for the classic field trials. So, to get the dog's attention, I fired my shotgun up into the air and got him to stop and turn around and tread water. Then I gave him a left-handed cast back to my imaginary X. But again the dog took off to the right, and I apologized to the people sitting in the blind with me. I was trying to impress them that this dog would do as he was told. And, quite frankly, I went to pieces. I hollered and I screamed and I blew two or three more whistle calls, and through it all he refused me.

"Then about seventy-five to one hundred yards way over to the right he came up with an old hen mallard. And I said, 'Boys, I was wrong. I was running a field trail blind to the X, but the dog was chasing a strong cripple and he came up with the meat.' I said, 'He's better at his game in this retriever business than I am.' So, I decided right then and there I was going to quit the classic field-trial circuit and start a hunting retriever club where the dog is encouraged to use his own head – to turn off the handler when the handler's wrong."

And not only is that a great example of what a hunting retriever should be, but it's also a revelation into how the hunting retriever

Hunting Retriever Club founder Omar Driskill poses Pup in gateway. He throws dummy north of fence while out-of-sight helper throws dummy south of fence as Pup is making his first retrieve. Since he can't penetrate the fence, Pup cannot switch birds.

clubs were started. For it came to pass that Omar Driskill became the founder of that movement in 1983.

Later that day, sitting in that Louisiana dribble, sipping tea, Omar also said, "You know, Bill, that was the greatest hunting retriever that ever lived. And when he died, I wrapped him in my hunting coat and buried him right out there by that fence. What a shame it was. Here was a champion hunting retriever that went to his grave, and there was no organization to accredit his skills, to post for all time in the record book what he had done and what he could do."

Well, such a record book and such organizations exist now. It all came about because of a dog that thought for himself and told his handler – whom he loved very much – to nevertheless take that whistle and shove it.

Swimming against the Wind

No retriever will willingly cast into the wind. He'll take the initial cast and then drift off. Or if sent at an angle to the wind, he'll not crab to hold his line, but instead will drift with the wind and the current. So here again, we don't cast the dog to get the poultry. We cast him to avoid the hazard, which is the wind. Consequently, we cast him where he can run with the wind – if possible – to the blind. Or at least run (or swim) some angle downwind. But judges know this. So they have the land hazard to the right – Pup touches shore, he's out of the trial. And the wind is blowing in from the left. So every time you give Pup a left-hand *over* to get him away from the land, the wind pushes him back.

It takes a very seasoned, very bold dog to hold his line in such circumstances. It takes, quite frankly, a field champion.

Handling the Diversion Bird

This problem could just as well have been brought up when we discussed land blinds, but it has applicability both there and here. While Pup's either going to get a bird or is fetching one in, a hidden (or visible) set of gunners throws a bird and fires; the bird lands in Pup's path, near Pup's path, or a long way off.

The point is, the bird is a diversion, thrown to *divert* Pup from either going out or coming in – to get him to change his intended line, which is the line given to him by his handler.

Because water is not Pup's element, he won't be so inclined to bend to the diversion – that would mean extra swimming. But on land, it's just a hop, a skip, and a jump over there, and a diversion bird can foul up Pup good.

So here's what we do. We practice – as always – on land. The handler heels Pup in a gateway, and a bird boy throws and shoots a bird on the north side of the fence. Pup is cast. Then while he's coming back, the handler or another helper throws a bird with a lot of hurrahing – make sure Pup sees it – on the south side of the fence. No way can Pup switch birds. So the handler yells, "Heel," and "Hold it," both commands being needed for Pup either may drop the bird or bolt for the diversion bird.

Once the land training has produced a fail-safe retriever, you just take the drill to water. No sweat.

Running Water

Running water to a retriever man (or woman) doesn't mean water running in a stream: it doesn't refer to current. No. Instead, it refers to shallow water that Pup can run in: he doesn't have to swim.

I mention this problem here, for this is one where the handler makes the mistake, not the dog. Running water is very noisy. Men don't realize this. So they blow for their dog to sit, and he keeps on running. That's one whistle refusal. As an old-timer once told me at a trial, "You're always permitted two mistakes before they throw you out." Should you whistle again and Pup not hear you, you're entering into that area of serious faults. And it's not Pup's fault. He's not ignoring you, he flat can't hear you.

So it's imperative the handler make himself heard. He must really lay into that whistle. And if it's evident the whistle won't carry, then the man has no alternative but to yell. Which is fine if hunting – and that's the supreme game, that's what it's all about. But yell at your dog at a field trial and you're out of the game.

One alternative is to try to get your dog into swimming water as quickly as possible. You can whistle him down fast. But what if the whole thing's a swamp? Well, nobody ever said it would be fair. And running water fits that category.

Hunting versus Trialing

Nowhere is the difference between hunting and trialing (even the new hunting retriever test format) more heightened than when it comes to water. And that's made even more critical by the water blind and the cold water blind.

Let's take a typical hunting scenario. The duck is shot and lands fifty feet down in the water, some five feet from shore. The hunter will cast the dog to run down the bank, leap in, fetch up the duck, and bring it back. This dog cannot be faulted. He's there to conserve game, and that's exactly what he just did.

But let's take the same shot duck at a field trial. Now the handler must send the dog by water to get the duck – the dog cannot run the bank. Why? Because by definition this is a water test. The duck is in the water. Therefore, the dog will get it via water – and no other way. I know it's arbitrary, but aren't all games?

Or let's look at another one. You have a great J peninsula and your duck blind is at the top bar of the J. But the shot duck lands in the water just to the left of the curve in the bottom of the J. Well, the field-trial man will line the dog to the bird via water. The dog must swim the entire length of the peninsula. But not the hunter. He will get out of his blind, cast his dog down the peninsula (the land), then cast him over to jump in the water to pick up the nearby duck. One fetch is sensible – it's an acting out of God's way. The other way is contrived – it's an acting out of man's plan.

So never, never argue the two. One is getting the meat; the other is getting the silver. The two of them have very, very little in common. One dog is trained to hunt; the other is trained for sport.

The national hunting retriever clubs that were born in the 1980s try to bridge the gap between the sporting dog and the hunting dog. And they're doing a pretty good job of it. But the tendency in sport is always to get more sporting. So I can see where the hunting retriever clubs will one day be running nonsense performers. That is, dogs asked to do tasks that wouldn't be considered in a day's hunt. I hope I'm wrong; right now, these clubs are the only salvation for the hunting retriever. If they fail, our great upland and waterfowl dogs will disintegrate. For like Omar Driskill's old warrior he buried in his hunting coat, there will be no place to accredit them.

Knowing When to Handle

The handler is part of the dog/man team. A very important part. We've seen above when he should be excessively loud in running water, and when he should keep his mouth shut to deal with a journeyman dog that turns him off. At all other times, he must think ahead for the dog, try to steer him from hazards, and predict what the dog's going to do. He should work out the consequence of such an act and either abet it or nip it in the bud.

I think now of a dog leaving the casting line and taking a wrong direction directly offshore. Well, if you hit this dog too soon with the training whistle, you will intimidate him. There have been just too many bad things happening in each retriever's life at shoreline. But here's the paradox: the longer you let that dog proceed in the wrong

Mike Gould casts Pup from fourth row of dummies in looking glass drill. Pup runs to the distant dummy pile, makes fetch, and returns through the corridor to the handler.

direction, the more convinced the dog will be in his mind he's right. Then you'll play Billy Hell trying to get him to switch course.

So handling is part art, part science, and mostly common sense mixed with a great rapport with the animal you're handling. This is why field trials are so exciting. Once you know how to read a dog, and you know what a handler's doing, you can predict what's going to happen.

I remember a field trial I ran in 1966. It was up in Minnesota. One of the pros in the open was trying to handle a dog – we'll call him Nemo – on a water blind. The other pros were all lounging around a kennel truck, and I think it was D. L. Walters who said to Joe Schomer, "One more whistle and he's going to lose him." Sure enough. The whis-

Now Mike casts past the corridor, and Pup threads the needle to make his retrieve.

This is the important part: Pup goes back same way he entered. This drill is very important for water work: Pup learns to take critical angle-water entry, plus come back to deliver to hand via the same route.

tle came and the dog bolted into the tules. That pro was driving around those field-trial grounds five days trying to find Nemo.

The handler didn't know when to shut up, just as other handlers don't know when to whistle. Like the Mississippi river boat gambler. We've all seen him. We've all met him. This is the guy who tries to wish his dog through a water blind. He wants to line the blind so bad (no whistles or hand signals) that he contorts his body, trying to put body English on the lay of the land and the mind of the dog – all to get the dog to do his will. But no. The dog's going to do *his* will. And that will is to go to shore. The man won't blow his whistle, for that would be a demerit, so the dog ends up on land. He's completely out of the trial now – all because the guy gambled.

In dogdom, gamblers never win. If you see your dog's confused on a mark or a blind, then sit him down with the sit whistle and begin to handle him. Make no nonsense about it, and let the dog know your commitment. The dog's made one mistake – he mismarked. Don't make another mistake by wishy-washy handling and have the dog turn off a whistle command or ignore a hand signal.

By the same token, if you're out hunting and you see Pup go left when you think he should go right, give him the benefit of the doubt. He has the nose and the ears and eyes and brains to have greater knowledge and insight of the bird and what he's doing than you ever will. Honor that. Encourage that. Develop that. Don't throw a wet blanket over it. A dog's not the one over whom you should show authority. He's one you should throw in with and encourage and pay attention to, so you might learn something about the wild.

Running a Straight Line

Most retrievers must learn to run a straight line: it's not imprinted at birth. Even on a flat field some retrievers will have a bow in their line from point A to point B. This must be corrected, especially on the retrieve. For the dog must come back the same route he went out.

Once again, retriever wizard Mike Gould of Carbondale, Colorado, comes to our rescue with his looking glass drill. You lay it out as follows.

Get yourself a handful of big, stark white dummies and go to a mowed-grass field – a flat one. Drop a dummy, take three steps in a straight line and drop a second dummy; take three more steps and drop a third dummy; finally, take three more steps and drop a fourth dummy. Turn around and look: the dummies must point in the same direction and must be in an absolutely straight line.

Walk fifteen steps at a right angle to this row of dummies and drop an identical row of four dummies. You've built an eight-dummy corridor some nine yards long and five yards wide.

Now heel Pup between the first two dummies – they're seven and one-half yards to his left and to his right. He stands in the middle; there are no dummies before him, but there are six behind him. Got it?

Okay, leave him there and walk out twenty-five yards and plant a pile of bumpers. Now go back to Pup, toss a dummy into the pile, and cast Pup for the retrieve. As he goes out, you walk back to stand between the two dummies in the second row. When he delivers to hand, wheel him about and cast him, again, for the pile of dummies. This time Pup sits with two dummies before him, two beside him, and four behind him.

As he makes his second retrieve, you move back between two dummies in the third row. When Pup delivers and turns around, he has two dummies to each side of him, two behind him, and four in front of him. Cast him for the planted bird. As he makes his way, you drop back to stand between the two dummies in the fourth row.

When Pup returns, you're standing in the fourth row of dummies, and when he delivers to hand and turns around, he'll be confronted with six dummies in front of him and one dummy to each side: there'll be none behind him. Cast him for the bird. But as he goes for this bird, walk five, ten, fifteen, or so yards behind the corridor of dummies. Now when Pup delivers to hand, he'll turn around and see the corridor for the first time. Cast him for the bird. He'll shoot through the gap; he'll thread the needle. And that's what we talked about earlier, isn't it?

When Mike's finished with this drill, he's standing one hundred yards behind the corridor and casting Pup to drive through the two parallel rows of dummies and out another one hundred yards to the bird pile. And this is important: *As Pup goes out, so he comes back—for he gets the same picture. And that's why this is called the looking glass drill. Pup sees the same thing coming or going.*

It's a magnificent tool. It teaches a dog to run a straight line by making the hazard the target. In other words, the object is to thread the needle, and the hole in the needle has always been the hazard for you and Pup, right? Well, this quite simply solves it all.

Should Pup go wrong anywhere en route, yell him down and get to him and heel him to the center of the corridor, then run the test again. The reason I say "yell him down" is that Mike starts this drill with his dogs before they're put on whistle signals. In other words, Mike goes to the looking glass drill before he goes to the baseball diamond: before he ever teaches the dogs to handle.

Now for that angle water entry.

You know the problem this can cause Pup and us. Well, just lay your dummies out on the bank—running into the water—and you can teach Pup to take the most radical water entries you can devise. Then remove the dummies and run Pup on the drill, and he'll follow the ingrained pattern. You can even lay out three corridors of dummies, one angling left, one angling right, and one straight ahead. Then carousel Pup about you on the casting line and cast him where you want him.

This is a take-off on the old wagon wheel drill. You stand Pup in the center of a circle of dummies and heel him about until you decide to cast him for one particular dummy. Now you start with four dummies, but before you finish the drill you can have sixteen or twenty-four dummies in the circle really delineating Pup's line. You can have Pup so refined he'll take casts of five degrees separation between the awaiting bumpers.

Now know this. After several weeks on the looking glass drill Pup will start to look for it. That's when you phase it all out to never return. That's right. You never go back, unless you have a Pup that's self-destructed and you must return to the basics.

Marking off Guns

The new hunting retriever format differs in many ways from the classic field trial's philosophy and techniques. The field-trial man stands as he runs his dog. But the hunting retriever handler duplicates a day's hunt afield, which is usually spent sitting, and so he must run his dog from a dove stool.

You'll have to work Pup on this. There's some confusion in converting from a standing to a sitting handler.

Also, the field-trial man never handles a gun. But the hunting retriever handler must. Now there's a reason for this. People who train with brutality generally shoot Pup with bird shot to get him to mend his ways or else they'll shock him in the neck with a remote-controlled electric collar. The preferred method of torture today is the collar. And these handlers object to anyone on line holding a gun, for they fear that's the way they trained their dog – by shooting him – and they don't want such trainers to have a preferred advantage. Sickening, ain't it?

We'll do none of this crap. We train with our head, not our hand, and the most brutal we are with Pup is swatting him with a plain white plastic flyswatter or picking him up and mock-mauling him and laying him on the ground to straddle him and tell him exactly what we think of him. Which is – as I've said before – the exact way momma dog trains. And she's the greatest dog trainer of them all. Why not imitate her?

Hunting retriever trainer Omar Driskill starts dogs on marks with a distant gunner. A bird boy (out of sight) throws a bird, the gunner to front fires, then Omar releases Pup to work dragging a short leash.

Okay, the handler now sits on a dove stool with his retriever heeled beside him. In the old days, the dog would mark the gunners and bird boys afield—and you'll recall the difficulties caused by this. For example, the dog may turn away from the mark before it hits the ground.

But now the gunner makes a weather vane of himself and the extended gun—he stays low so Pup's almost looking down the gun barrel. In other words, the best of all things is happening: Pup's marking off the gun. He's looking down the barrel that kills the bird at a test hunt or a day's hunt in the field, and he has every advantage in marking. Nothing could be finer.

So how do you teach this?

First off, you seat yourself on the dove stool and call Pup to heel, sit, and stay beside you. The bird boy is far afield with a bird or dummy. Immediately in front of you and to the right is another gunner sitting on an identical dove stool. When Pup looks to field, he sees this offset gunner and the distant bird boy.

Now you, the handler, signal for the bird to be thrown and *the obliquely placed gunner shoots it.* In other words, he stays low and dramatically makes a pointer of his body and the extended gun, and Pup looks right through him to the falling bird.

Then as the days proceed, this gunner is brought closer and closer to Pup. Finally he's no longer used. Only the handler has the gun, and he does the firing while Pup looks straight down the barrel.

It finally gets to the point where you really don't have to place your hand beside Pup to line him on a mark or a blind. He marks off the gun and institutes his own initiative.

Also, note this. The hunting retriever handler must hold his gun throughout the test. So practice this way. Don't put your gun down. You usually don't while hunting; you've got it ready to kill the odd bird that chances by while Pup's out working.

And yes, when you go to doubles or triples you can put three gunners out before Pup, or just one gunner who does all the shooting. Or you can have one gunner shoot two of the birds and you shoot the

Omar eventually handles the gun himself. He makes his body a weather vane so Pup marks off the straight line of the gun and the gunner's arm and body. Note that the check cord is clamped under the gunner's feet so Pup can't break.

Ty Trulove uses more conventional form in getting Pup to mark off a gun. You may want to lower yourself even more so Pup has the gun in his field of view.

third one. Finally, just as in hunting, you shoot all three birds from the dove stool.

Now follow the sequence. Call for the right-hand bird. Partially raise and extend your body and push out your gun to make a true marker of body and gun, and fire. Then call for the left-hand bird: but Pup's sitting to your left, and often times you must physically move him with your left hip to shoot this second bird. Fine. Pup stays in close and looks right down your body and your gun barrel. Then you call for the third bird and do the same. When all the gunning's done, look at Pup to see which bird he wants first, then tell him, "Back," either using your hand cast or not. When Pup returns, he'll place himself in line for the next bird he wants. Honor that and cast him. Same with the third bird.

So that's it. We've confronted the problems that can plague a retriever and corrected them. Now we move on to flushing dogs. I don't
know about you, but I've had a lot of fun doing this. And that's what
you and Pup should be having. Correcting problems shouldn't be a
grudge match. It should be a thoughtful reconstitution of Pup's mental
approach to the bird, gun, and field. There are few dogs that can't be
salvaged. And I hope your Pup's making the progress intended when I
put all these things on paper.

PART FOUR

THE FLUSHERS

13

The Flushing Dogs

THE FLUSHING DOG is a vest-pocket edition of both the pointer and the retriever. He is asked to quarter (both the pointer and retriever do) and find game (ditto), which he flushes (the retriever will do this). Then he waits for the gunner to fire (both the pointer and retriever do) and fetches up deadfall or takes the hunter to where the covey landed (ditto). Consequently, in the preceding pages we've already corrected most of the flushing dog's faults—though it is true they have some special problems all their own. However, some of these problems—such as range—depend on terrain; and where one dog is faulted because he has too far a range, another handler would say it's just right or not far enough (more about this later). Also, the flusher is one sporting dog that's expected to be rock-bottom steady. And he is especially designated the role of honoring without a flinch.

When I speak of flushers, I include the English springer spaniel, the American and English cocker spaniels, the Welsh springer spaniel, the clumber spaniel, the Sussex spaniel, the field spaniel, and any dog that will flush. And as noted above, the hunting retriever can now be included in this category as well as many an errant pointer that knocks birds up.

Flushing gun dogs are mellow mates. Easy does it in training and handling. This is the ultimate dog you train with your head and heart — never your hand.

The English Springer Spaniel

In dawn's soft wash of light, we hunt the North Dakota prairie for sharptail grouse and Hungarian partridge. Sheila, an English springer spaniel, maintains a constant beat at gun range before us: casting twenty yards right, then crossing twenty yards left. She hunts head up, searching for the bird's scent. Then her tail beat quickens, her head goes down for foot scent, and she vacuums the carpet floor.

She's on to something. . . .

Running laterally to the left, she suddenly raises her head (she's deep into the birds' scent cone now and shifting back to body scent), and she leaps to have the prairie erupt before her in a rocketing of twenty-five Hungarian partridges. The birds are too fast for me, but professional English springer– and cocker spaniel–trainer Tom Ness, of rural Bismarck, North Dakota, drops two, and Sheila is cast to fetch the near one.

Taking the bird to hand, Tom says, "She's just past a year, Bill, and she's learned all she just showed you through experience – not through discipline. I do no negative training: everything is positive. I let my dogs do what they can so their natural instincts come out – their natural ability.

While an English springer spaniel is coursing for game far to left, handler Tom Ness tosses a pigeon to the right in moderately heavy cover.

Springer crosses the field to scent pigeon and in he dives: wingbeats clapping in the cool North Dakota dawn. This is the ultimate prize for the flushing dog handler: the vigorous flush.

"I encourage rather than discourage," Tom emphasizes. "Everything I do is to build a fire in the dog, not to control it. And that's the way you train a spaniel."

"That's the way every gun dog should be trained," I tell him.

"Yes," replies Tom, "but with the springer it's imperative."

"Why's that?"

"'Cause they're so soft, so sensitive. The harshest correction I can make on a springer is to run out there yelling and pick up the dog by the scruff on each side of its neck and tell it how disappointed I am in it."

Pup comes charging from the field and the handler toots a whistle, raises his hand like a traffic cop, and commands, "Hup."

Then the handler takes a step in the direction he wants the dog to cast. Coaxing the dog to scat with upraised arm, he says, "Hie on."

Pup is centered in the great doorway to the puppy fetching pen. Tom Ness fires the puppy up by bouncing and scooting a dummy in the grass. Then the dummy is cast (see, it is still in mid-air), and Pup is allowed to break to build up enthusiasm.

"I do that," I tell Tom, "but sometimes on the real hard-headed ones I lay them down on their backs and straddle them and shout down in their face – the way their momma does when they're pups."

"Wouldn't work on a spaniel," I'm told. "Anything that harsh and they'd sure quit you for the day . . . and maybe quit you for life."

"Then, if folklore has a Chesapeake Bay retriever as tough as a cast iron kettle," I joke, "you say an English springer spaniel is as fragile as fine crystal."

"That's right," Tom agrees. "But that's good. It means the average man can train one. That is, if he approaches the job with love and tenderness and play and good times.

"Like me. You know how I get the dogs on birds? I let them do it. I take them to field, and as they run before me I dizzy pigeons from my gamebag and toss them to ground. The dog doesn't see me do this, he's casting to the left. But when he sweeps back right, he runs directly into the bird and it flies away. That excites him, fires him up. And if he chases . . . that's okay. That teaches him he can't run down the bird. And if he happens to catch the bird, that's fine, too. I call him back to me with the bird in his mouth, and he's learning to retrieve. That's what I mean. They're trained with experience, not discipline."

"What else do you do?" I ask.

"Well, I never teach obedience for the first year. But the dog naturally learns to give to the lead, for I'll walk them on lead for over a mile a day. The longer they walk, the more comfortable they get, and the more they relax. Then they just naturally walk at heel from then on.

"There are very few commands for a springer. *Hup* means to stop, sit, and stay. *Heel* means to stay beside my heel or come to my heel. And *hie on*, or *get on*, means to cast — and you emphasize that with your body, stepping sideways and arching your body and casting with your arm.

"And never let the springer learn the power of the gun too early. Let them chase and chase and chase. Finally that out-of-sight chase will shorten to seventy yards, then to forty, then finally the dog just

Pup wheels about with dummy in mouth and heads to the handler—not to deliver to hand, but to see if he can outflank the trainer.

quits on his own. But if you were to shoot one of those birds, the dog would believe that *sometimes* the bird does come down, and he'd go on through life wanting to chase.

"So, the gun is saved until later. You start by clapping your hands to resemble the bang of a gun; later, you fire the standard .22 blank training pistol."

"Well," I ask, "what's the result at a year's age?"

"I have a dog that hunts hard, retrieves right to hand. He quarters back and forth; he turns on the whistle command; he comes back on the whistle command; he's steady to flush and shot – and all his experience has been on pigeons.

"Then hunting season opens and they're ready. And I try to get them into as many wild birds as possible. When the season closes and winter is upon us, that's when I do my strict obedience training. But by then I've got such a fired-up dog, he's become interested in learning; he doesn't resent my curbing his freedom. He figures everything from now on means more birds. Now when I blow the whistle for the dog to

Tom Ness starts Pup hunting by teasing him with a fluttering pigeon, which is then cast to cover.

turn at quarter, he turns, and when I blow the whistle for him to hup, he stops and turns to stone — even if I throw a bird right over his head. That's what I mean by discipline."

I interrupt, saying, "Okay, I'm with you in all you say. I agree with your methods and I salute your approach. But can we put all this in a linear perspective? My readers would like some sort of timetable — though they realize that all depends upon the trainer, the dog, and many other variables."

Tom thinks a moment, then answers, "Let's put it this way. The raw puppy starts his retrieving in a three-sided enclosure, going for a dummy, and I give a hand clap for noise.

"Then the started pup retrieves dummies right up to my hand, or on my lap when I'm sitting on the ground. Here's where we make introduction to feathers and gun noise. I let him chase, and when he's far distant I fire the gun.

"The started pup and I go for walks, and I introduce quartering with whistle and hand signals. I start rolling the dummy in front of the

Tom tells Pup to hup *and stand his ground. Then he is immediately cast for the fetch.*

pup so he is starting to find something to be running for. He is beginning to hunt. I always match the cover to the pup at this time. Nothing
frightening. I want that pup to think he can run through any cover
easily. Tough cover would only discourage him.

"Okay, now we'll move on to the seasoned puppy. He retrieves,
quarters, turns, and comes back on command. He will also heel and
hup on lead. He can find and flush birds from cover. Does not chase
unshot birds out of the country, but does retrieve those that are shot
and fall. This dog can be hunted, if care is taken not to shoot too much
game over him. We don't want him to unlearn the sequence: the birds
get up, the gun goes off, and the bird flies away.

"Now we have the finished puppy. This is a seasoned pup that has
been steadied to wing and shot and introduced to water work. At this
point, I would determine if I had a field-trial prospect or a gun dog.
Two things are absolutely critical for trials: perfect mouth and a bold
flush. There is no difference between the training of a gun dog and a
trial dog up to this point. In fact, there is no real difference in the
training all along. We run the trial dogs much shorter lengths of time
trying to teach them not to pace themselves: keep the fire!

"Now for the started dog. This is a finished pup that has had some
experience on game. He quarters, he's steady, he retrieves from land or
water. He has also had extensive obedience work and will hup, sit,
stay, and heel off or on leash.

"Finally, we arrive at the finished dog. We've given our started dog
a season's experience on game. And we have taught him to do blind
retrieves in the manner of the classical retriever.

"With every class, I follow a natural progression for the introduction of game. I go from the frozen bird to the dead bird, followed by
the wing-clipped bird and then the live flier. It's the same in all my
training. I want the dog to master one step and become confident in his
ability to do it before I move ahead. In other words, I make sure he
doesn't mouth the frozen bird before I let him touch a cold, dead one. I
try to let the dog 'learn' as many things as possible before I start to
interfere and impose my own will on him."

"Fine," I tell Tom, "we'll keep this all in mind as you go on talking."
I then ask the thirty-seven-year-old former welterweight amateur
fighter, "Why would anyone want an English springer spaniel?"

"They're the best there is on pheasant," I'm told, ". . . and rabbits.
Actually, they're a dense-cover, a punishing-cover dog that has to root
out the bird or the hare. The pointer would point from afar. The
springer digs the bird out. He'll cast into this silver buffalo berry here,
and it's tangled and thorny. He'll come out all roughed up, lips bleed-

ing, thorns stuck in his nose, but he'll not quit. He'll keep hunting.

"And he'll retrieve ducks on a warm-water hunt. But you'd need a Lab when the season gets cold.

"Yet the springer is a do-it-all dog as well. She got the Huns up, didn't she? And she'll get the sharptail up, too. You'll see. And she's used for ruffed grouse and prairie chicken and even bobwhite. But the springer's speciality is pheasant. For pheasants like to hole up in inaccessible places, all buried in a pile of tumbleweed for example, and this dog will kick them out.

"Plus, there's this. Every gun dog hunts but one or two months of the year, but the other ten or eleven months he should be a house pet. None finer than the springer. He has the disposition to be close, not to tear up the place. He'll also mind and show lots of affection."

"Tell me," I say, "how do you get the dog to work so close to you? Not to get out of gun range?"

Tom explains: "A pointer works for the bird . . . but the springer works for the gun. From the start of training, the dog learns he always finds birds close to me – I'm throwing them from my gamebag – and I

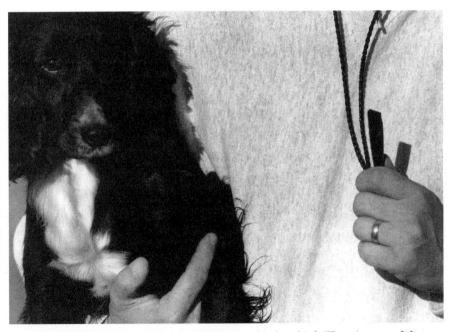

The staghorn whistle makes the plaintive cry of a shorebird. There is none of that raucous blast of the pea whistle, which would startle game.

make sure there are no wild birds ahead for him to stumble on. Success breeds success. I'm the bird producer . . . the dog gradually learns if he wants a bird he must get close to me . . . and automatically he stays close.

"Of course, he's on whistle and voice commands. He gets too far out, I call him in; he gets too far to side, I stop him and cast him the other way. But the main thing is that birds and me, in the dog's mind, come to be the same thing.

"And I don't just throw those dizzied pigeons anywhere. They're usually cast into the rough stuff—like snowberry. Consequently, the dog learns the bird is always in the thick stuff, plus the bird's always close to me. Then, too, when the bird flies away the dog learns he can't catch it. Plus, as he's chasing that fly-away I fire the blank gun once or twice so he's being taught the sound of the gun without becoming gun shy. The dog just learns that if he doesn't hunt by me he doesn't find birds."

"And why that staghorn whistle?" I ask. "Why not the standard pea whistle?"

"It's because of pheasants and rabbits. To them, nothing is more disturbing than noise. I can take you out here the third week of the season and get out of the car and slam the car door, and we'd see the birds running through the field to the end of the cover and away they'd go. We want to keep the noise to a minimum. For nothing seems to be more disturbing than noise—especially noises the birds associate with humans.

"This is a plastic Acme 210½ whistle that costs two dollars, and it comes from England. It makes a high-wind noise the dogs can hear but the birds don't mind."

"Is there anything else about equipment that's unique?"

"Not exactly. It's just the opposite. There's some equipment used by bird dog people you'd never use on a spaniel. Like a mechanical releaser—a catapult launcher for birds. The way these dogs drive in and flush game, it wouldn't do for them to crash into a metal contraption. It would stop them cold. They'd never drive again. And that's their value.

"So you train a springer with birds. Tons of birds. Not equipment. And if you're training a gun dog, and not a trial contender, the spaniel is one of few dogs you can train alone. You need no help. And that's really an asset. You do it all yourself. Just walk the dog across the field and toss out birds. Simple as that."

As we continue the weekend's hunt, I grow more and more proud and delighted with the springers put down before me. There's John Staley from Grand Forks, North Dakota, with his springer, Rivington.

The most popular gun dog in America today is the English cocker spaniel. When you buy your pup make sure it's from field-bred stock.

And the big Norwegian Vince Hjelle from Bismarck (if he were a silo, you could store a year's supply of grain in him), and his yellow lab, Katy. They all work well. But the springer's animation, his joyfulness, his determination, his happiness with his work is to be admired. I know the dogs produced every bird within range. I know I missed every bird they produced. But John Staley and Tom Ness and Vince Hjelle are master shots, and they harvested enough for a groaning table.

The English Cocker Spaniel

Compact cars have taken over America's roads just as compact gun dogs may dominate our bird fields tomorrow – and, surprisingly, for the same reasons: more scat, less fuel, easier upkeep, smaller storage, greater control, and on and on.

The most popular AKC-registered purebred dog in America today is the American cocker spaniel (ACS). He leads all other breeds of dogs in both litter and individual registrations. And though the ACS's heritage is bird hunting (after all, his first name was *woodcock spaniel,* for his ability with this bird) still, bench enthusiasts have essentially ruined him for the field.

But during the past few years, I've heard rumblings in the distance of the rebirth of the field-bred cocker in America. He is now imported from England (English cocker spaniel: ECS). And he comes to us with all the intensity, birdiness, hard drive, hunt, and water love that typified his old-time American counterpart. The ECS in America has by now a handful of proponents who are going all out to make this compact gun dog a contender for best-of-honors in the American bird field.

Take the Reverend Walt Cline, for example. Remove eighty pounds and you'd have another Gary Cooper. That same innocence of face, the wayward tuft of hair hanging over the forehead, the gentle timidity, the slow and measured way of having his say. Walt is a thirty-six-year-old, small-town preacher from Morrill, Nebraska. Poor as a churchmouse, totally without sense of self, nearly a zealot in his love for dogs, Walt's been a bird hunter since he was a fourteen-year-old Nebraska farm boy. He's risked bread and board to assemble the seven cockers that run through our legs as we head for water.

Walt tells me, "I wanted to be a game biologist or something out in the fields. But somewhere along the line I heard an inner voice tell me there was more eternal significance in directing a man's soul to God than in saving another canvasback duck. Yet," he grins, "I've always kept the duck in mind."

The bumper goes in a high arc over the glistening lake and plops, and seven cockers leap, hearty as frogs, and pump madly for the fetch. Walt says, "I tried to do it with ACSs. And it can be done. But what a chore. Take Dolly out there, she's American bred. Oh, she'll hunt – you can always entice her with a bird. But field-bred cockers are more intense, have a stronger natural retrieving instinct. And they just tend to do more things naturally.

"American show-bred cockers have a latent ability that can be developed. To get Dolly, for example, to hold a bird I'd stand her on the table and put a bird in her mouth and praise her for holding it. It took hours and hours.

"And when I took her afield everything had to be immediately successful, or she'd lose interest.

"But the ECSs jump out of the crate hunting – and they don't even know what they're looking for. Plus, their instincts seem to intensify as they grow older."

Walt talks and the pack swims back, trying to drown the one dog with the bumper – leaping over each other, going under, cavorting, and yes, laughing. What Walt says about cockers is worth our attention. He's paid his dues, having told me, "My take-home pay was $160 a week, but I had to have this ECS and the price was $750. He was supposed to be started. And he was worth it to me, for I had a full litter-brother of his that got killed and I knew what the blood could do. So I sold all but two of my shotguns and an old hunting pickup I had and bought the pup."

On another day Walt revealed, "My first two ECS imports came in the same crate and cost me $1,269, including air freight."

But he explained the sacrifice, saying, "Here I saw this magnificent little gun dog going down the tube . . . becoming a lawn ornament, if you know what I mean. And I was saying, 'Somebody has to do something. Someone has to save this blood.' But then I remember that's what I'm always telling my congregation. When something has to be done, do it yourself; don't stand there saying, 'Why doesn't somebody do something?'"

The dogs are leaping about us now and shaking water and running to dry their faces by rubbing them sideways in the sparse grass. Walt points out, "Show-bred dogs have characteristics that are a hindrance to field work. Look at Dolly. Her coat is not suitable for the field. I can show you pictures of her with snowballs all bound up under her legs. And I was picking her up, breaking the snowballs off, and it was terrible – the mallards were really flying, and there I was messing with a dog that had the wrong coat for the field.

"But Whisp and Daley, my two English imports, didn't have more than a couple of little balls and those in places where it wouldn't hinder them. Turn Dolly over and look under her armpits – there's a lot of hair in there that matts, and it has to be trimmed out. But Daley, in those places where he rubs, has no hair. And just as important, there's no hair in his ears.

"The show cocker's ears set real low on the head, and they are so long they've become tubelike. This shape and the excess hair encourages debris to work up and enter the ear canal. This is especially bad since the cocker may be working below seed level in the field. But the field-bred cocker has his ears set up on his head, the ear is flat – not like a tube – and there's no hair on the inside to transport debris.

"Plus the show cocker's feet are too hairy. Always need to be trimmed. Not with the field-bred. Also, the texture of the hair is different: the field-bred cocker's hair doesn't collect debris.

"But the big advantage of ECSs in general over American cockers is their eyes are set deeper in the head. Americans have gone for Bambi eyes. Consequently, there's more eye surface to collect junk. The dogs are pop-eyed, which means they can be easily struck by something in the field while running.

"So tight eyes, good field coat, naked ear, ear conformation that mitigates against debris entry – these are the desirable characteristics of the ECS. But most important is their intensity, their desire. And they have the biddability to learn, or else you'd just have a sky rocket. Plus, there's more fun to an ECS if you do it in water. They just make great retrievers. And they'll retrieve all day.

"There seems to be less consistency in size in field dogs than in show dogs so when you buy a show dog you get uniformity in conformation and a great disparity in ability. You don't know what you're going to get. In the field-bred dog you've got uniformity of ability and instinct, and some disparity in conformation. A small bitch could weigh only twenty pounds, field-fit. Could be as short as fourteen inches at the withers. That's absolutely tiny. A large male could be eighteen inches tall and weigh forty pounds. And that's solid muscle.

"But again – apart from all that – the field-bred cockers have great quartering, driving, hunting, and birdiness instincts the show-bred won't necessarily have."

And that pretty well sums it up. It's not me talking, it's Walt Cline talking, and the nation's bird hunters talking. Show-bred stock just isn't fit for the job. I don't care what breed of gun dog it happens to be.

The Total Training Program

Now that we've met the English springer spaniel – the most popular of the spaniel group and the one that serves as their gun dog representative in America – and the English cocker spaniel, let's get into detail on just how the spaniel is trained. Then we'll look at the problems this gun dog can present.

Tom Ness has shown us that the mainstay of training is to walk the dog afield – what we would call controlled Happy Timing – where the dog learns the only birds he's going to find are close to the gunner. Thus, the dog hunts close to the gun. A pointer can range a quarter of a mile, and if he's staunch on game he'll have the bird penned down by the time you get there. But the English springer spaniel is going to do it himself. When he finds birds, he busts birds. So he can't be a quarter of a mile out front. He can't be more than thirty yards – by the time you shoot the bird, it is forty yards. And that's the range of most shotgunners. And there is this. Mike Gould, up front with his miracle Lab named Web, told us of one-hundred-yard casts. Well, again, a Lab works different than a spaniel. Gould can tell when Web's making game and whistle him down. Not to point, but to stand and wait. Then Mike comes forward and either flushes the birds himself or casts Web on in to do it. Plus, there is one other factor. Web hunts in the mountains, down in deep ravines, off cliffs, if you will; he can be one hundred yards up or down, yet if he should flush birds, they could still fly within range of the gunner.

So springers are close-working dogs. That's all there is to it.

And thus they must be trained for just that. And totally for that.

Fetching

Springers (and remember this applies to all spaniels) should be started in training by fetching. Tom Ness has a novel way to accomplish this. He's built a three-sided, eight-by-eighteen-foot chain-link pen, and he kneels in the "doorway." The puppy is held to side and excited by bumping the dummy about, so that it scurries and leaps over the dog's approach. Then, when Pup is looking, the dummy is thrown to the far end of the enclosed pen. Sure enough, he'll return with the dummy on the first fetch and attempt to skirt the trainer – to escape to open field.

But Tom catches Pup and entices him once more with the dancing dummy, then tosses it again. Now the bright spaniel will go get the dummy, but he won't want to come back. What fun is that? He got this thing, and now this guy wants to take it from him. So the enterprising

Pup tries to dig out. But Tom is cajoling and whistling and clapping his hands, and finally Pup relents and comes back with the dummy. One or two retrieves is enough for a young pup. Any more than that and he'll lose interest; and that destroys all you're trying to instill.

Later, Pup is given a frozen bird, then a thawed bird, then a warm bird, and finally a live bird. Such a program teaches Pup always to come when called, always to hunt close, to learn there's no escape afield, to understand the bird, and to realize the real joy of the game is pleasing the handler by delivering to hand.

Happy Timing

Springers are started afield by taking the dog on lead. There's a reason for this. Naturally, the dog will want to bolt, to go search the wild world, to investigate all those strange scents, to leap at the grasshoppers, to dig in the gopher's soft earth mound. If given such freedom, the only way the handler can curtail him is by voice. And nagging will put a springer off his game faster than anything. Even all-age gun dogs are brought to line in a field trial or taken to the field to hunt on lead so the handler is hassle-free. No need starting off the event, or the day, by yelling at the dog. The lead dispenses with all possibilities of this.

Once afield in training, the dog is released to hunt. No way he'll vacate the country now, for there are live birds in the handler's game vest that he continually dizzies and rolls into the cover. This is an opposite approach to teaching the dog to quarter by outfitting him with a twenty-foot check cord. That was my initial training method, and I've recommended it in my writing. And it can work. But I've now learned that running the dog free keeps the fire in him: fire that you can take out, but not put back. Neither does the dog drag a check cord to control his outward pace. He runs free, totally free, with only the birds to keep him close.

The handler throws a dead bird if he wants a retrieve; a live one if he seeks a flush. Now there is a way to roll in a live bird.

First, you take the bird in hand with wings collapsed to the body and you vigorously twirl the bird's head horizontally. Then you drop the head straight down and twirl some more vertically. Enough of this, and you throw the bird to skim across the grass, say, ten feet away. You don't want the bird to bounce, for this can revive him. Plus, there is this to know. Pigeons get wise. Four or five tosses and they immediately get up and walk away. They've become dizzyproof.

For training value, this bird can now be pinioned so he can't flush, and the pup can retrieve a bird.

So here's the scenario. The springer is casting before you, and when he isn't looking, you dizzy and roll in a bird. When the dog crosses and he's downwind, he smells the bird, twirls, races forward, and leaps to catch it. The harder the drive, the better. No matter what happens, the dog is self-taught. If the bird flies away, the dog chases to learn he can't catch it. If the bird is caught, the dog is encouraged to retrieve it. Plus, the dog learns that the bird is always found in the rough stuff—for that's where you threw it. And the bird is always found close to the handler, for you only threw it ten feet away.

See how much better this method is than teaching quartering with the old check-cord method? You'll recall this is the way we control pointers. The dog races to the left, we give the stop whistle, or yell, "Ho." The dog twirls to see our outstretched arm, and we walk right with our right arm up. That's fine for pointers. They're tough and they've got a ton of forward drive. But not the springer. He's too soft. Too sensitive. Let him have his total freedom. Curtail it just enough—with birds—to keep the dog close and do your bidding. It is natural training, and I salute it.

Later, when the dog self-steadies, you can tell him, "Heel," and then, "Hup." Or you can give the whistle signals for these commands. One short, hard whistle blast means to stop. Two short blasts of the whistle means to sit and then change direction—but with a seasoned dog to just change direction without sitting. And one long, low whistle tells the dog to come in, or if the whistle is sustained, to actually come back to heel.

The Cast

English springer spaniel trainers were mightily influenced by sheep dog trainers. Matter of fact, I suspect many a midnight mating with a border collie went into the creation of the English springer spaniel. I believe that's where he got his smartness and his biddability. A more concrete example of sheep dog influence comes from sitting the dog down, walking away from the dog, turning around, then casting the dog sideways by saying, "Hie on," or "Get on." Retriever trainers and pointer trainers cast their dogs from their side—facing the field. But not the springer trainers. The field's behind the dog. Except on a blind retrieve—then the springer trainer does it the same way the Lab trainer does: at side.

There's a good reason for the side cast. Most casts on a day's hunt will be given during the process of finding game. And the dog is always cast away from the old fall. You don't want him hunting the same cover or getting hung up on old scent.

To actually cast the spaniel, the trainer makes sure he's hupped: that is, he's stopped, he's sitting, and he's staying. And to accomplish this, the trainer can stand before the dog and repeatedly say, "Hup," or blow the proper whistle command. Then the trainer takes a few steps in the direction he wants the dog to go, bends his body that way, and gives a long, sweeping arm cast in that direction as he says, "Hie on," or "Get on."

The dog immediately stands, turns, and runs in the direction he's been cast. When he reaches the limit of gun range, he'll turn out of experience. If not, the trainer must hit him with the *toot-toot*, and walking the opposite direction, give the extended-arm signal for the dog to get over—to reverse his field.

Together, the two of them—gunner and dog—lace the field just as you tie up a pair of hunting boots. Though the hunter takes but a few steps in directing the dog, the dog runs twenty to thirty yards in each direction.

To keep the dog happily working in what could be a monotonous routine, the trainer continues to seed the field with plenty of live birds—always to excite the dog, always to keep him hunting and driving and striving to catch the bird before it can loft away.

Matter of fact, it's the springer's desire for birds that trains him. If he were just ho-hum about birds, then the trainer would have to resort to the check cord to sustain the beat.

All during this field training, the springer is not given the yard training we gave to the pointer or the Lab. The dog has a year afield and one winter's hunt before serious discipline is attempted. And that's just heel, sit, stay, come, and so on. The same thing we teach the Labs, done the same way.

Now, we're training a gun dog spaniel, not a field-trial contender. If this were a trial dog, we'd need two sets of guns and two bird boys: one set on each flank. The dog would course between them; the bird boy would loft the bird, the gunners would kill it, and the judges would tell the handler to send his dog to fetch it up. Which, incidentally, is another way to get the dog (even if he's to be a gun dog) to quarter the field before the handler. He runs between guns.

Now Tom Ness advises, "When I start to feel the dog is really hunting well and has lots of drive in the cover, then I'll start a little more of a mandatory compliance. It's a gradual thing. It's not a line drawn in the sand. But let's say I've got a dog that I know I want to turn at the end of a cast, and she's got something going on other than a bird. If she's got a bird or some scent of game going then I never interfere, but if she's just futzing around over there and I blow my whistle to come and she won't, then I go over there and scold her. And very seldom do I ever get a dog that needs more than that. Her head goes down, her tail goes down. She is totally whipped, totally sorry. And she mends her ways.

"And the bird work gets more intense. After I got them hunting and retrieving well, I do my yard work. I get them to heel and hup. Then I start working really vigorously on hup. I'll blow the whistle and I start them across the field; then I blow the whistle right away to get them to hup down. Cast them and blow the whistle right away.

"And I do the old drill where I have them out afield and call them back—only to stop them half way. And then I start with the wing-clipped bird. I'll get the dog really going for it. I'll build that drive over the course of a couple of weeks so I can get this guy out here hunting in front of me. Then, when I throw a bird up, hit my hup whistle, shoot my blank pistol, he'll stop—even though he'd prefer to drive on for the bird.

"Then I hup them and throw the bird behind me. If the dog breaks, he's got to run right through me. Later, I start throwing the bird at angles ever closer to the dog. Finally, I'm throwing the bird right over his head and he's sitting steady."

Review

The first year is spent hunting and retrieving.

At one year of age (and this depends on each dog—never can there be an exact timetable) the dog is brought in for yard work, basic obedience, heel, sit, stay, and come when called. He must absolutely turn on the whistle and come back on the whistle.

When the dog is booming in on every bird and he's flushing hard, and he's hunting and retrieving well, then you steady him.

And that's where the dog is hupped and can't move. Then the trainer has the dog at heel and throws short retrieves, restraining the dog if he must. The bird is thrown over the handler's shoulder, which means he is between the hupped dog and the downed bird. Then, as stated above, the angle is altered until birds appear to side; finally, the bird is thrown over the dog's head to land behind him.

Then birds are produced, and the dog is driving hard to fetch them. The handler blows the hup whistle to stop Pup in his tracks. This is the ultimate test. And one that must be delayed in training until the last. Never would you right off the bat stop short the drive in a sensitive dog. You can understand why you wait months before you get to this point.

During the same one-year period, the dog is taken through his first winter's hunt, after which yard training commences in earnest. The reason? All the drive that will ever be in that dog has already been instilled. Now he can take some curtailment without giving up the spirit.

So that's a general review of training. Now, what are the problems a springer can present, and how do we solve them?

Any problem a pointer or a Lab can have will show up in some spaniel. But there are specific problems to the breed and to the way they must hunt.

Like the Labs and the pointers, the dogs can be hard on game. Not hard mouthed, exactly, but they can spike the bird with their canines. It will be a heavy thing for the dog to go to the magic table (see chapter 6), but that's where he's headed. Only, it is done with so much tender care. Understand? Of course you do.

Range

The primary problem unique to springers is they hunt too far from the gun. The way to handle this is with tons of birds – even letting the dog see you have a bird in hand. Keep him ever watching. Let him think he's outsmarting you. Dogs like to do that, you know. They love to beat you at your game – or think they did. Such a spaniel will keep his eye on you wondering when a bird is going to appear, thus giving up his forward drive and automatically hunting close.

But you also can have a springer that does just the opposite: he flat hunts too close. This is the dog that polishes your boots. To counter, you plant birds well ahead, and as you walk the dog into the wind he learns he must cast out to get into game. Remember, the excitement of the bird is what keeps the dog driving and hunting and anticipating. If the bird is always coming out of your hands, then the dog hunts close. But should the birds always be far to front, the dog extends his hunt.

It stands to reason the short-range hunter needs a wild bird season under his collar. The excitement of a covey flush – the delirium of seeing twenty or thirty birds loft and beat the wind all at one glorious moment. This will get the dog from under your feet. This will get him to hunting.

Now just a moment. I said above that the springer needs a year's hunt under his collar. Let's talk about that collar. The springer man is still using the choke-chain collar. To his credit, he uses a heavy one so it doesn't cut in so much. But still, it's not in my training program. I want you to use a wide, flat, plain leather or nylon collar with a strong D-ring.

It has also been discovered that some trainers will get a coughing dog because of the choke collar. So, they'll switch to the pinch collar. You remember what that is? That's a spike collar with the studs all filed blunt so when the collar is contracted (it tightens over a built-in roller) the dog is pinched by the angled studs. Once the dog complies and quits fighting, the collar goes slack and the studs pop straight back up to stop pinching.

I maintain that none of these collars is needed. As sensitive as a spaniel is, why put an instrument of torture on him? No, these collars don't qualify as instruments of torture in experienced and sensitive hands. But are those your hands? Have you had ten years of professional experience in gun dog training?

Pointing

A fault peculiar to springers that would be heralded in most other breeds is pointing. And pointing is really a tough problem to cure. You try to solve this problem by giving the dog a lot of wing-clipped birds – a lot of birds on the ground – so the dog continually catches birds. This will hasten up their closing in on flush.

The problem of pointing is probably based on pressure coming from the trainer who insists the dog hup after he's flushed the bird. Thus, the dog anticipates this and says, "I'll just avoid the whole mess by stopping short and looking at the bird." If the bird doesn't flush, so figures the dog, then he'll not get scolded.

And should the dog hesitate before the bird long enough, it will look like he's pointing – where he's really just postponing the whole process to put off getting jumped.

Besides giving this dog a lot of birds on the ground, you can also entice him to trail a duck. English call ducks are used for this, due to their nature of keeping a steady pace and not hunkering down like a pheasant. Plus, a duck is wide and he's brushing off lots of scent on the cover. Place the dog in sparse cover, introduce the duck to the heavy stuff, and let him go. Make the dog wait five minutes, and then cast him after the scent.

It'll be a long trail, and the longer it is, the more excited the dog becomes. When the dog reaches the duck, he thinks nothing about pointing; instead, he leaps right in for the catch.

Blinking

Blinking a bird is usually an extension of pointing. Somewhere along the line the trainer has put on too much pressure, especially on being steadied. So the dog's avoiding the consequences that go along with the flush by pretending he never saw the bird. You treat this problem the same way you do the pointing springer. Either keep the dog in wild game or have him drive in hard on lots of roll-in, wing-clipped pigeons.

Cast Refusal

Another problem for the springer is he won't take a cast. Tom Ness tells us, "For a dog that knew what I wanted and was just refusing to do it, I'd blow the whistle, yell, and rush over there to him. Then I'd pick him up by the scruff of his neck and tell him to stop that silliness. Then I'd set the dog down and walk back to where I was and cast him. When the dog got just about by me, I'd hit the turn whistle again. Right away the dog must turn the other direction, and if he doesn't—he's close enough to me I can get to him fast.

"It's the same with the come-back whistle. I use the come-back whistle a lot of times as a range adjuster. When I cast them off, I bring them back from forty to sixty yards, and then I give them a side cast one way or the other. And if they don't answer the come-back whistle, I get out there fast and tell 'em what I think of 'em."

And that's about it for springer problems. Spaniels are really easy dogs to train and keep tuned up—that is, if you don't apply pressure and you keep your coop filled with lots of birds. Springers can't take pressure. They won't take it. But birds will keep them happy.

They're the perfect dog for the Tarrant method of training, where intimacy, and not intimidation, is brought to bear. Where we train with our head and not our hand. Where we give the dog (or puppy) that sufficient freedom to self-train. Where everything positive is enhanced and nothing negative is ever laid upon the dog. And if some freedom must be removed from the puppy or dog (and it must be), then the dog is immediately sweetened up, immediately loved, immediately placed in a position where he's successful so he doesn't see the world as an anti-dog place.

14

From Head to Tail

WELL, THIS BOOK is finished, and in the writing of it and in the reading of it we've learned a lot about dogs – and ourselves. For let's never forget the human equation. Remember "I've never seen a bad pup . . . only a bad dog." And what happened to that dog from puppy-hood to dogdom is us: Man!

We also learned it is a lot simpler to avoid a problem than it is to correct one. And we learned as well so many truly important things: 1. There can never be a timetable in training a dog. They're all different, we're all different, the two of us together make for much uncertainty. 2. There's not a problem that can't be solved with birds. And maybe that's why the springers are so carefree, so problem-free. They are trained only with birds. And that might be a good solution for all breeds. 3. Nothing bad can ever happen to a dog that he can associate with a human being. 4. Train with your head, not your hand. Train with intimacy, not intimidation. And in this regard, possibly the springer should have started off the book, for his sensitive nature demands a hands-off approach. And that's what we've proposed for all breeds. 5. When in doubt on how to train a dog, place him in a position where he self-trains. Better yet, turn the job over to other dogs. Nothing can train a dog as well as another dog. And we know we're not talking about the dog being aware of it. Remember the chain gang. 6. Let each dog have his puppyhood, it may well be the most delightful time of his life for both you and the dog.

In every case, we trained a healthy dog with no congenital deficiencies. Also, no dog was trained where the field and birds or the hunt and quest were bred out of him for the show bench. We assumed in each case we had a bona fide gun dog pup to start with. Anything less would have defeated us. You can take a show-bred dog and spend a year on him and accomplish (usually) what you would have done in a month with a field-bred specimen. Nowhere is this more graphically displayed than with the spaniels. The English springer spaniel and the English cocker spaniel have no peer in America. The show bench has destroyed their Yankee cousins. So you must go back to England for the hunting blood in those breeds. And there you must be careful. For they have dog shows in England, as well, and these dogs are rendered unfit for the field.

So that's it. We've caught the early morning sunrise together at the duck blind and felt the rough brush scratch our pants legs as we coursed for upland game. We've won some and we've lost some. And in the end, I guess it finally does boil down to this one last thought: a trained dog is that dog that has only those faults the trainer will put up with.

Heh?

See ya down the road.

Index